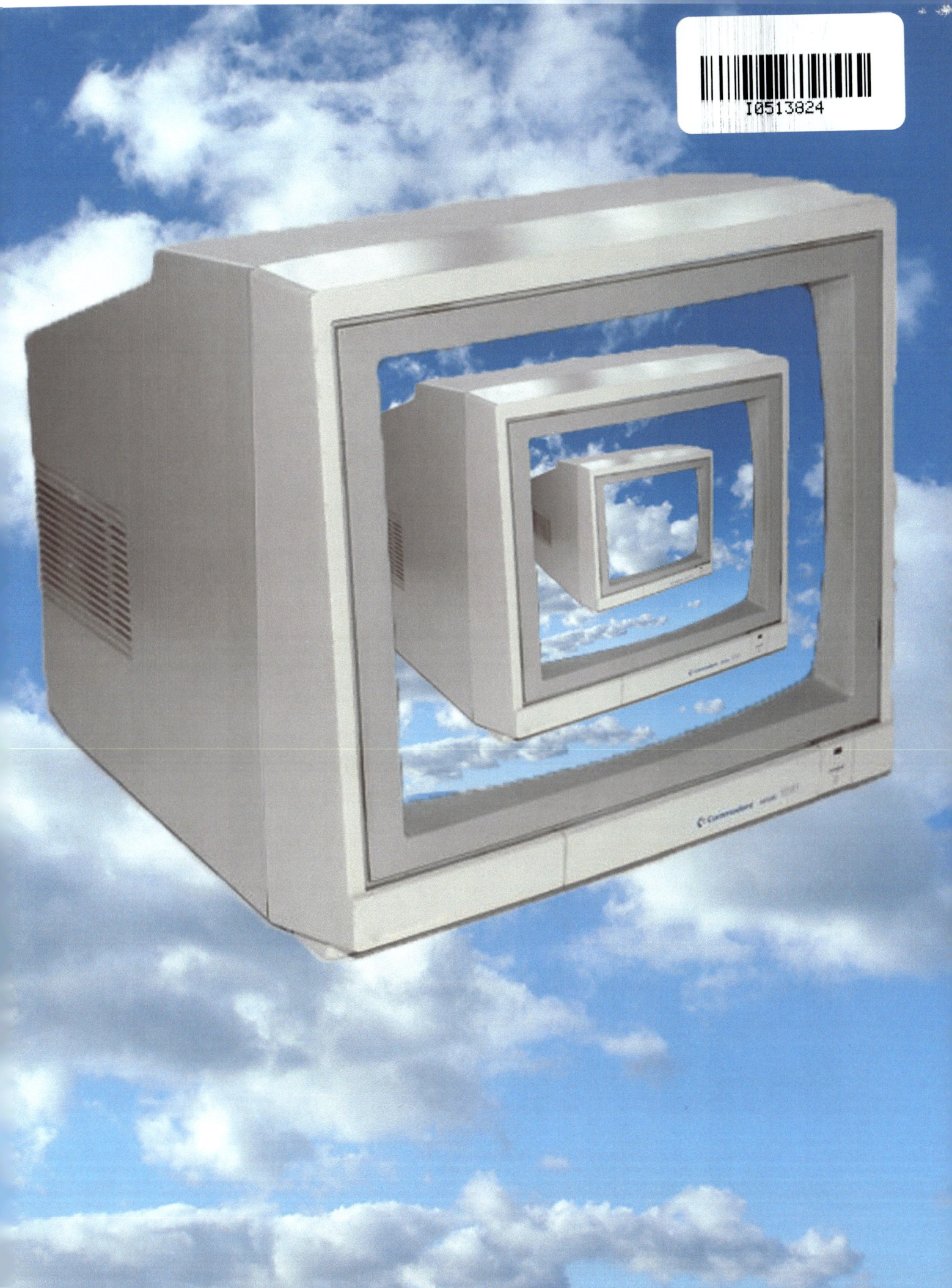

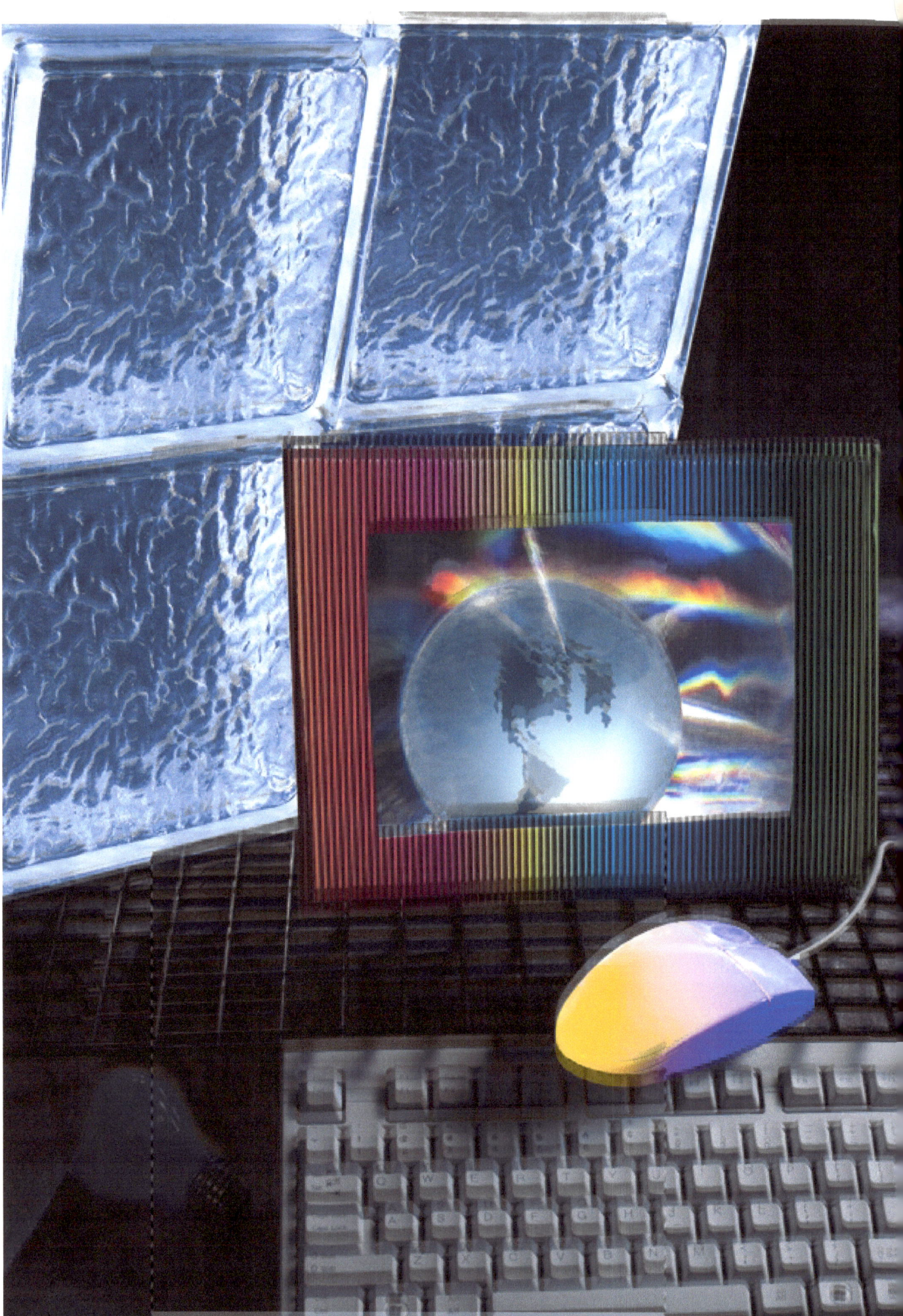

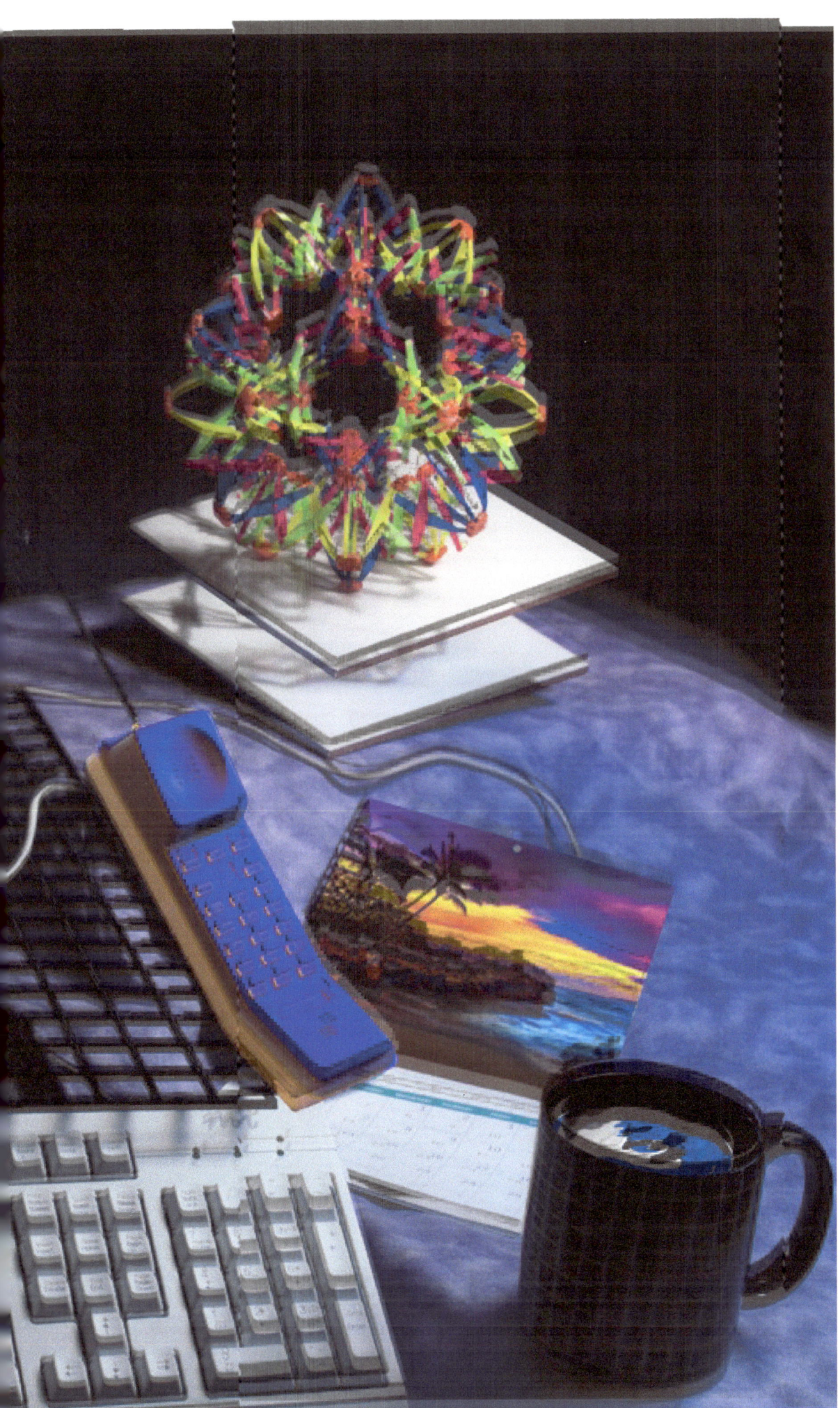

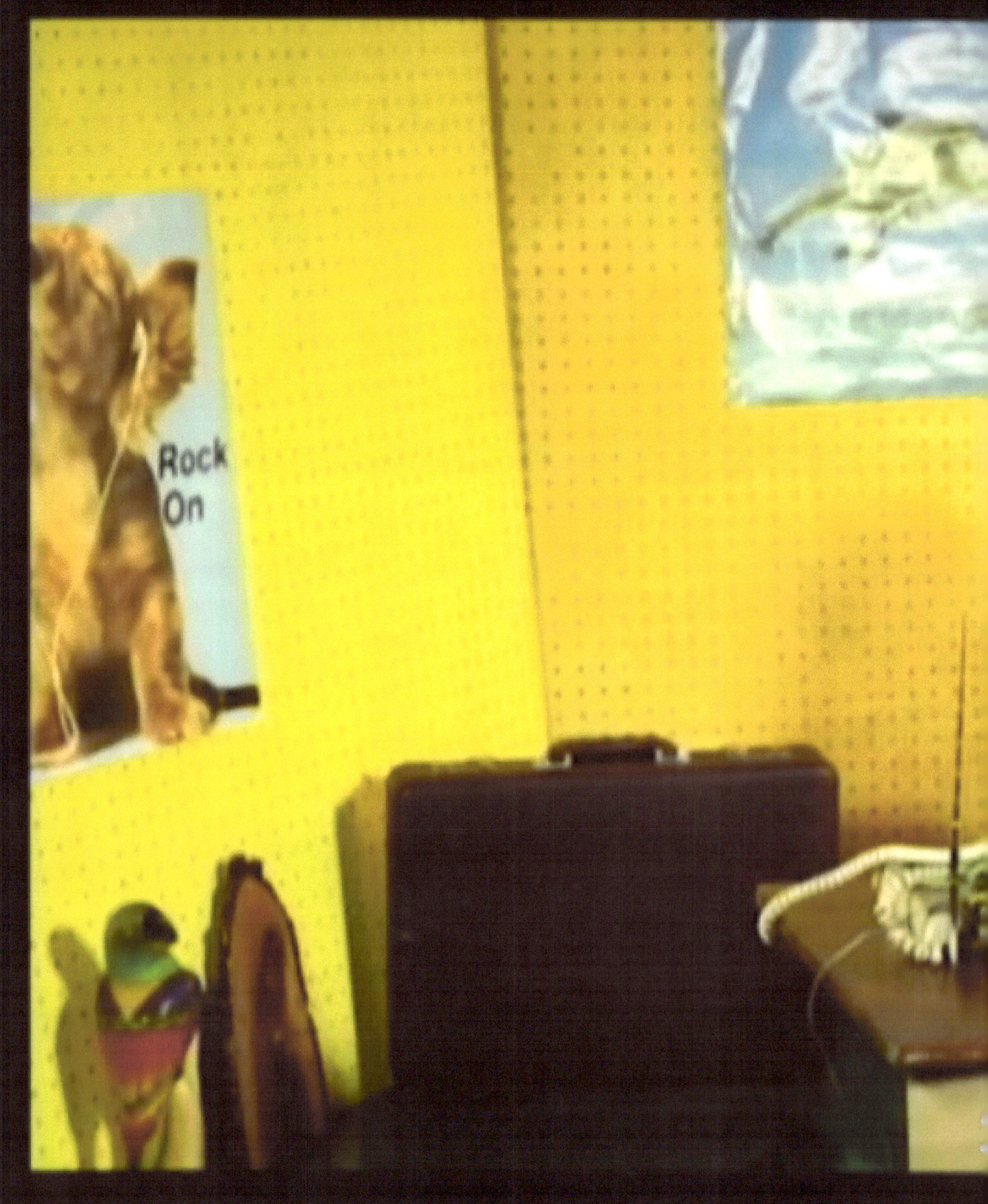

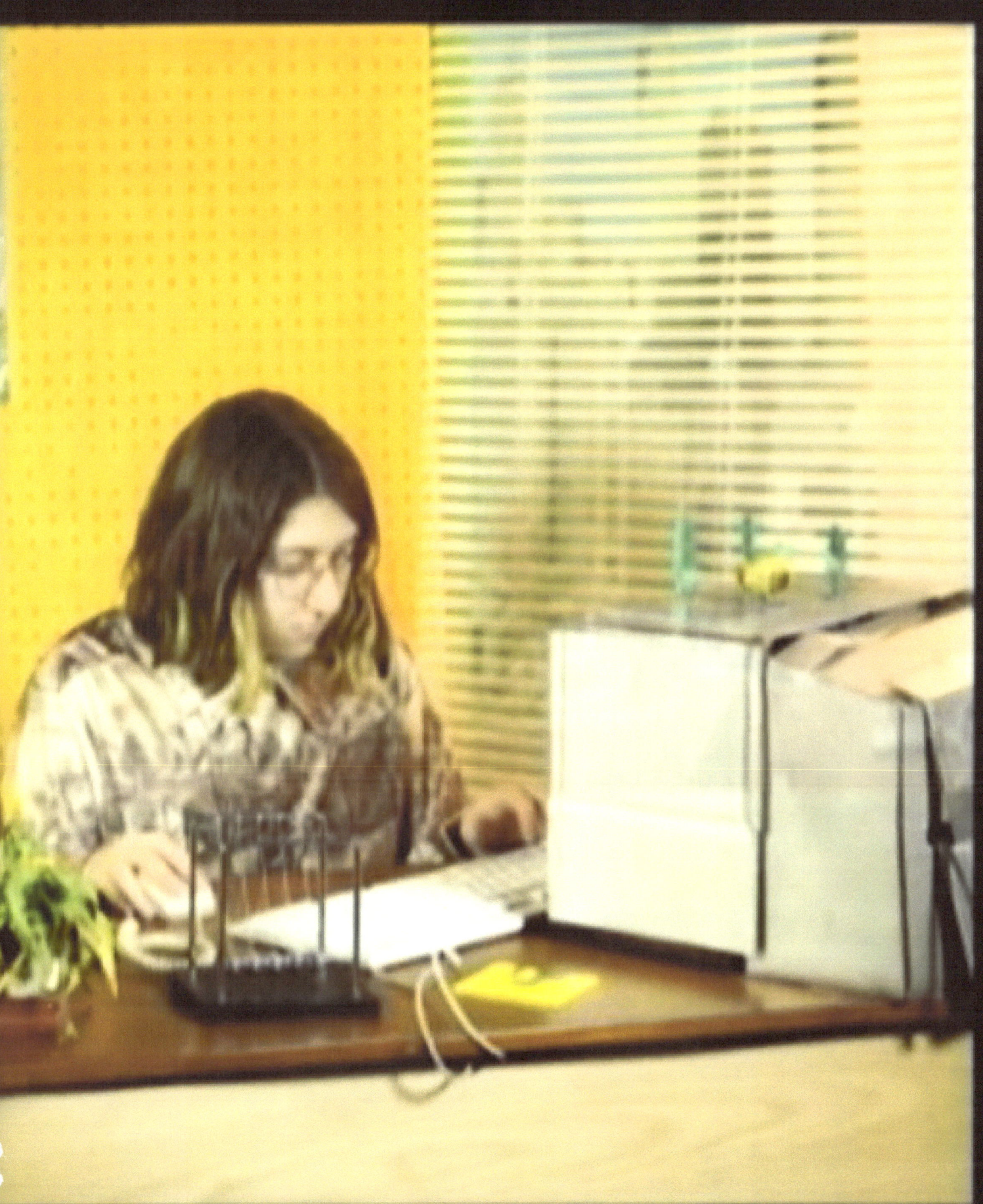

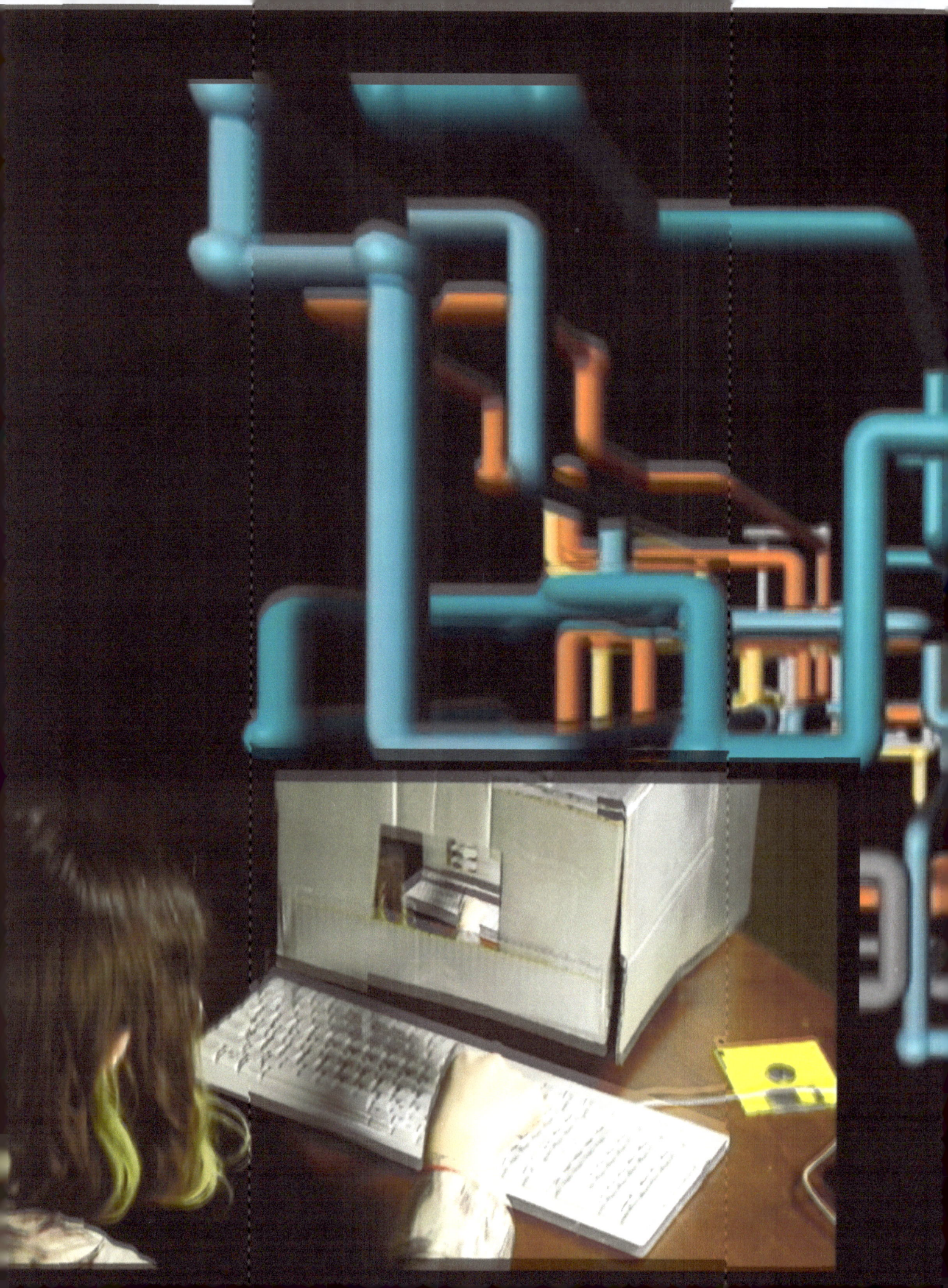

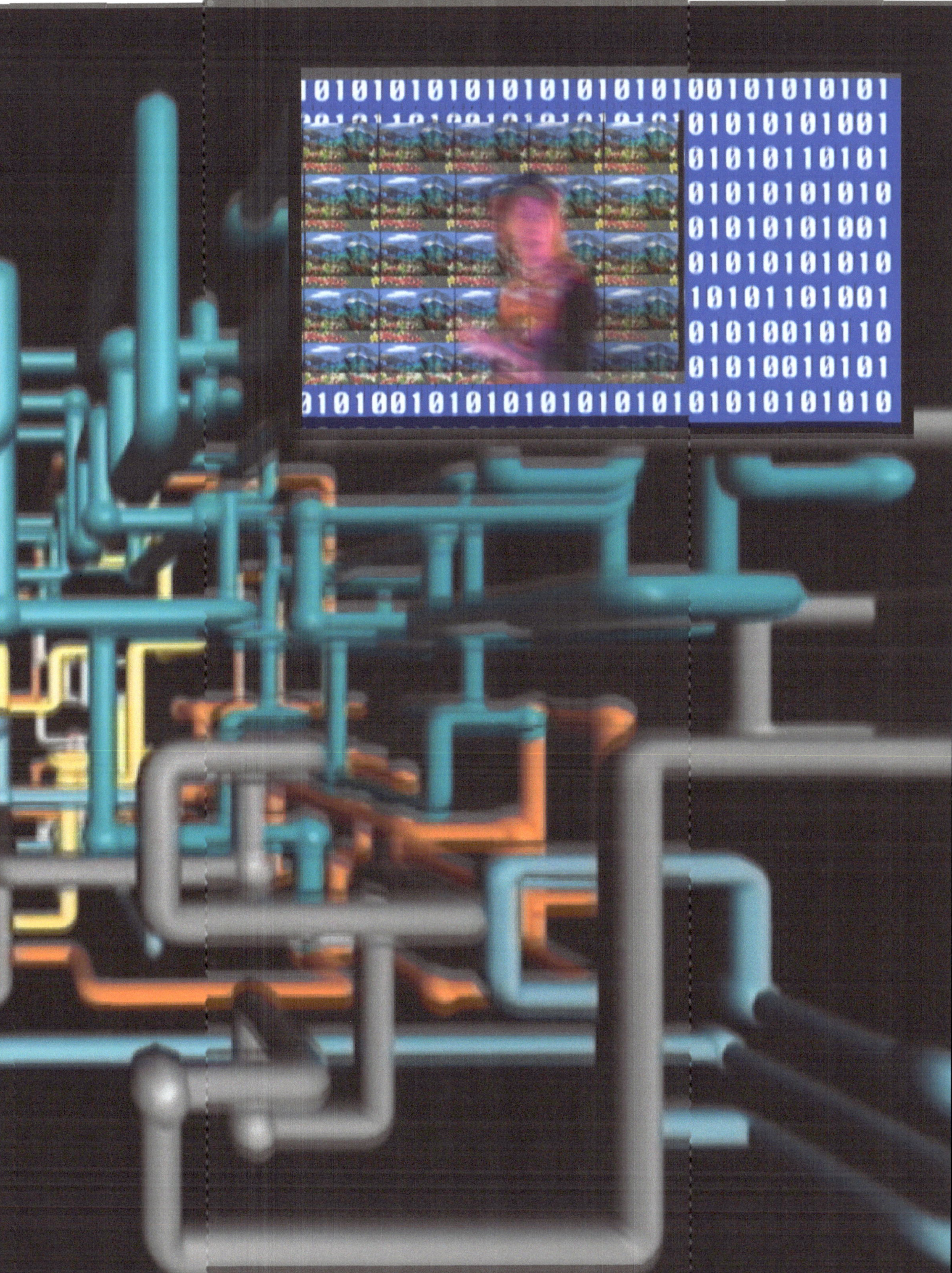

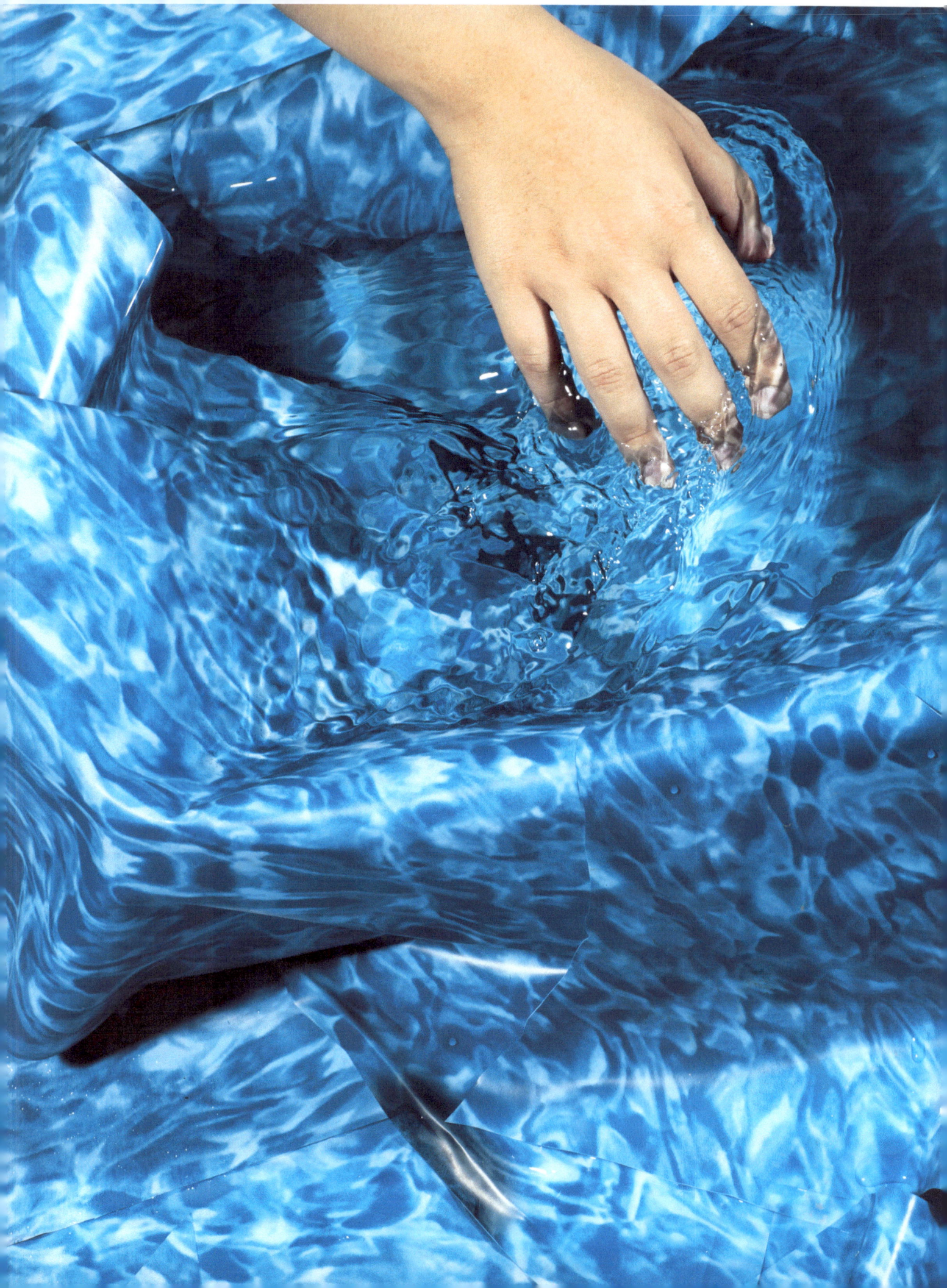

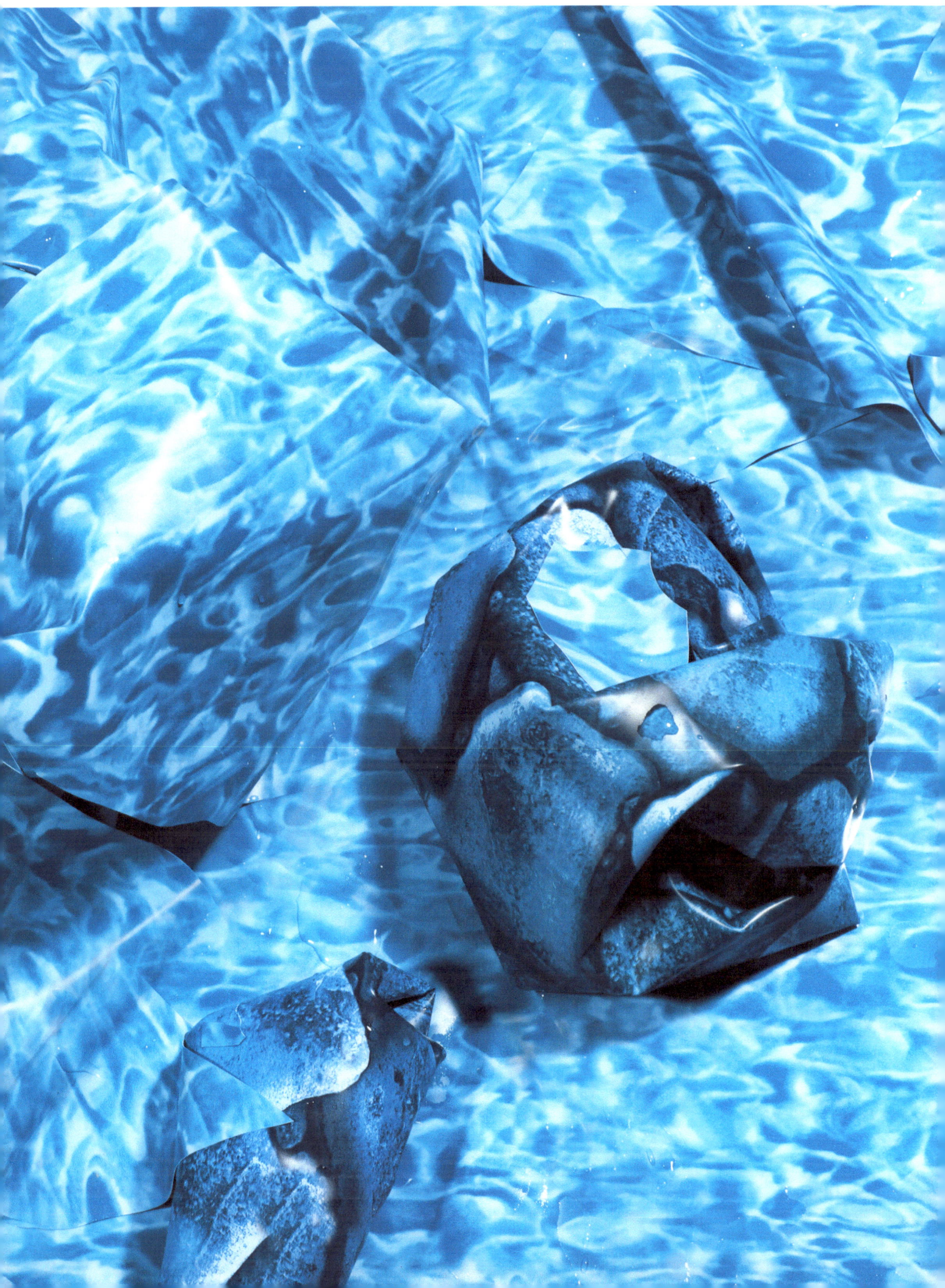

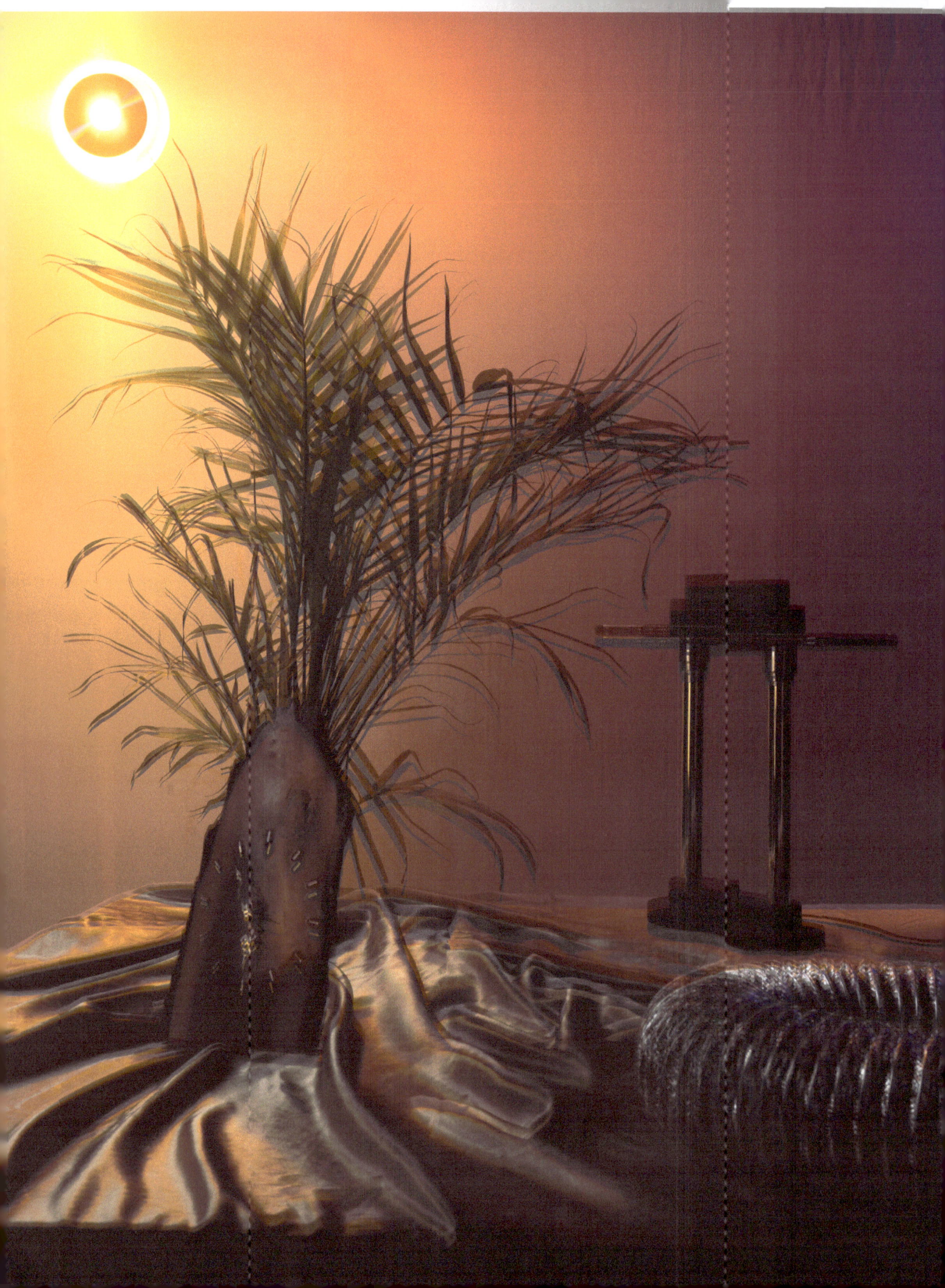

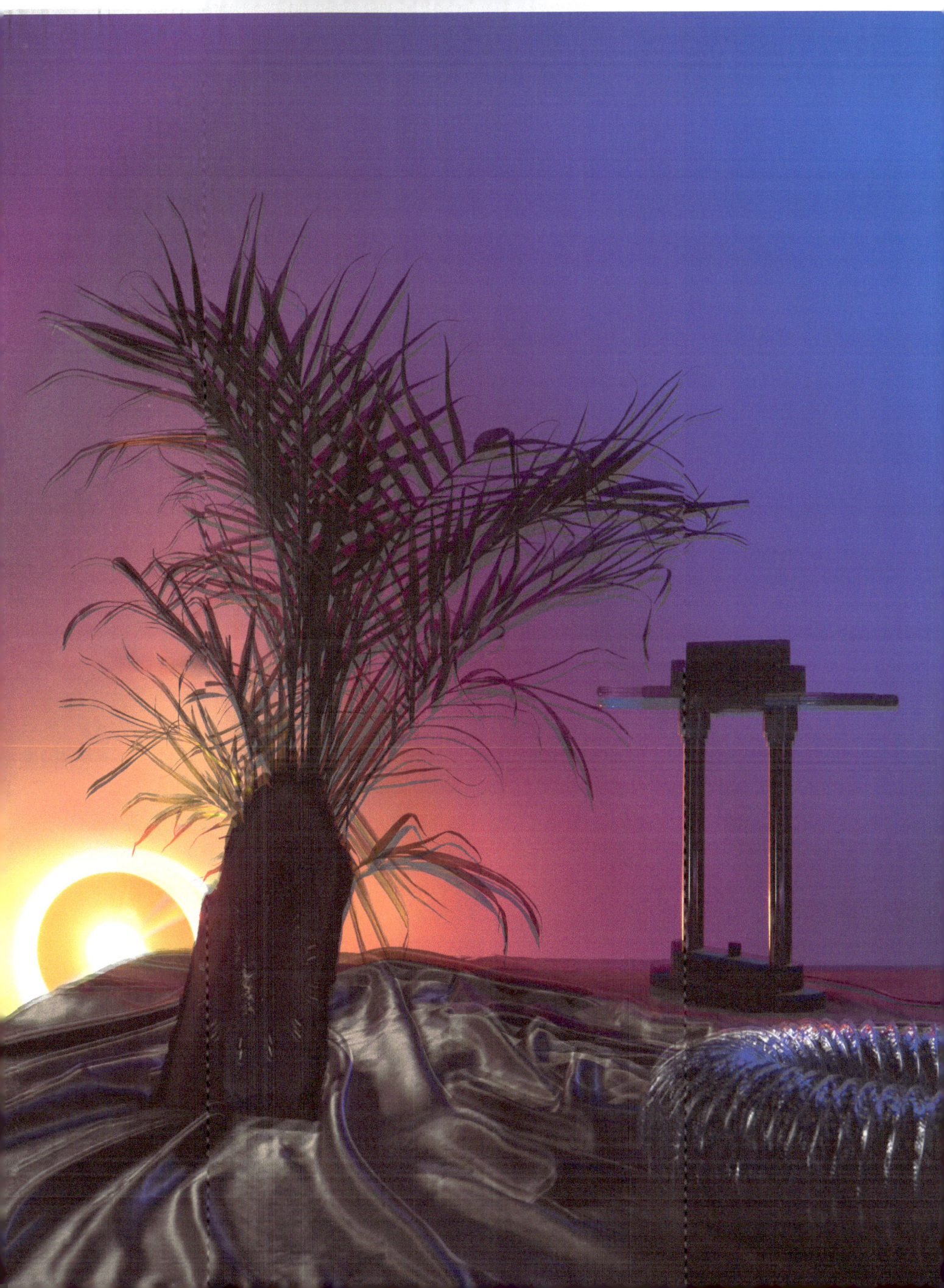

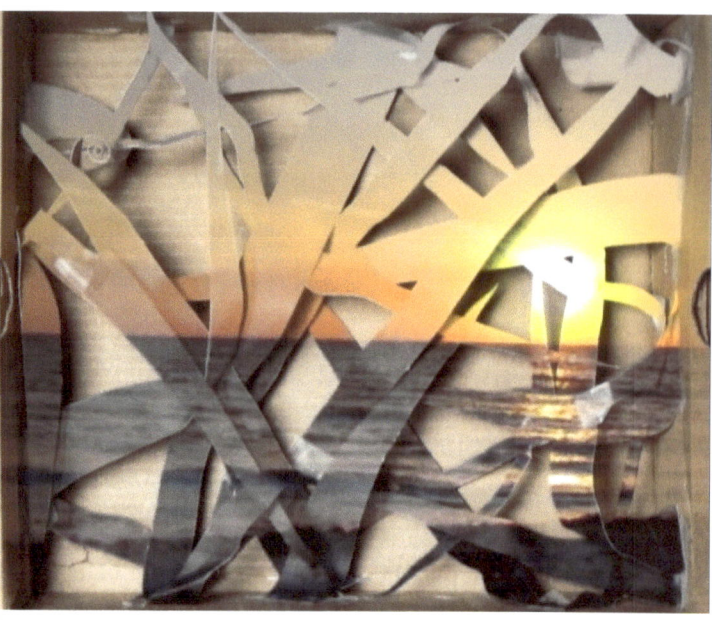
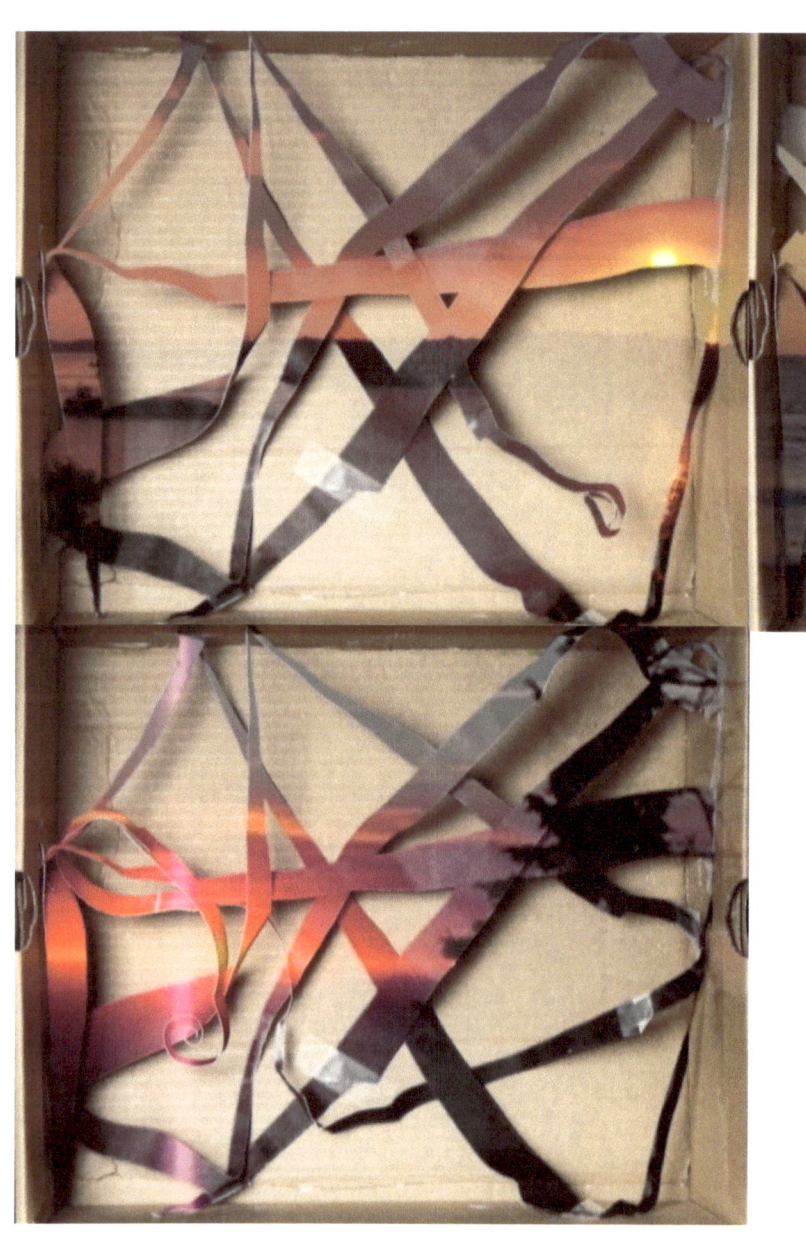
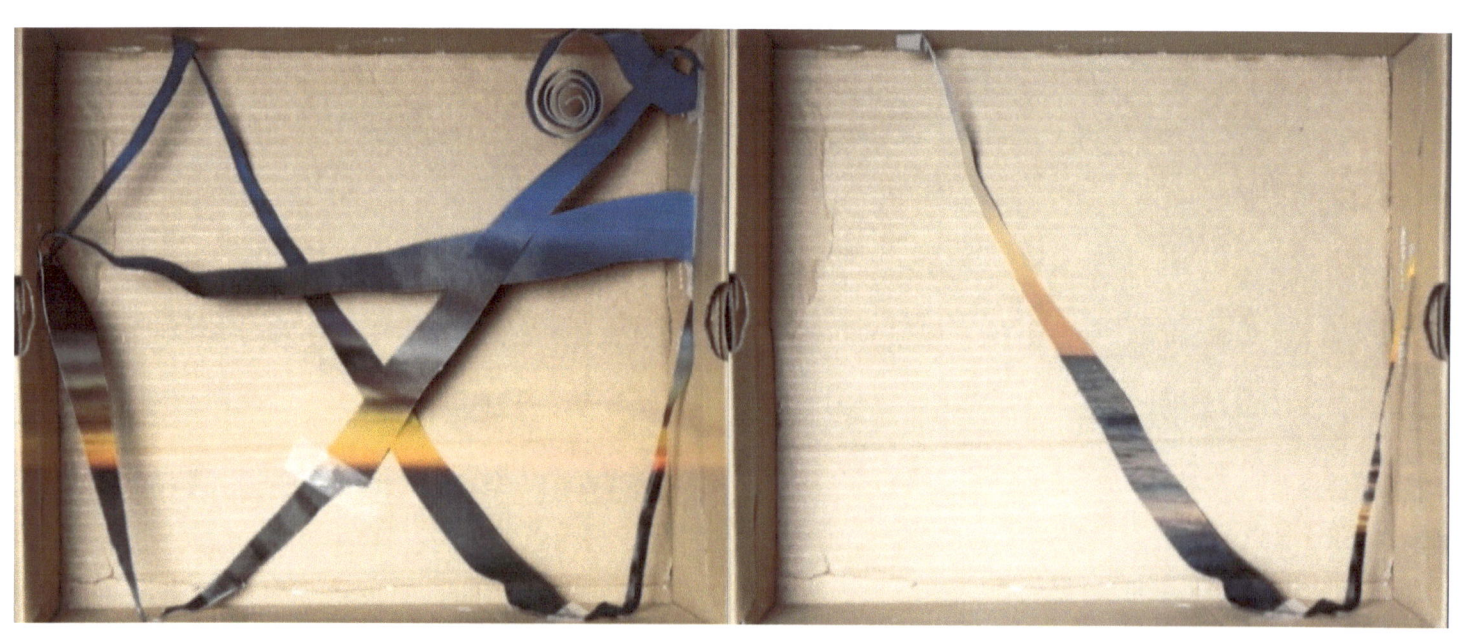

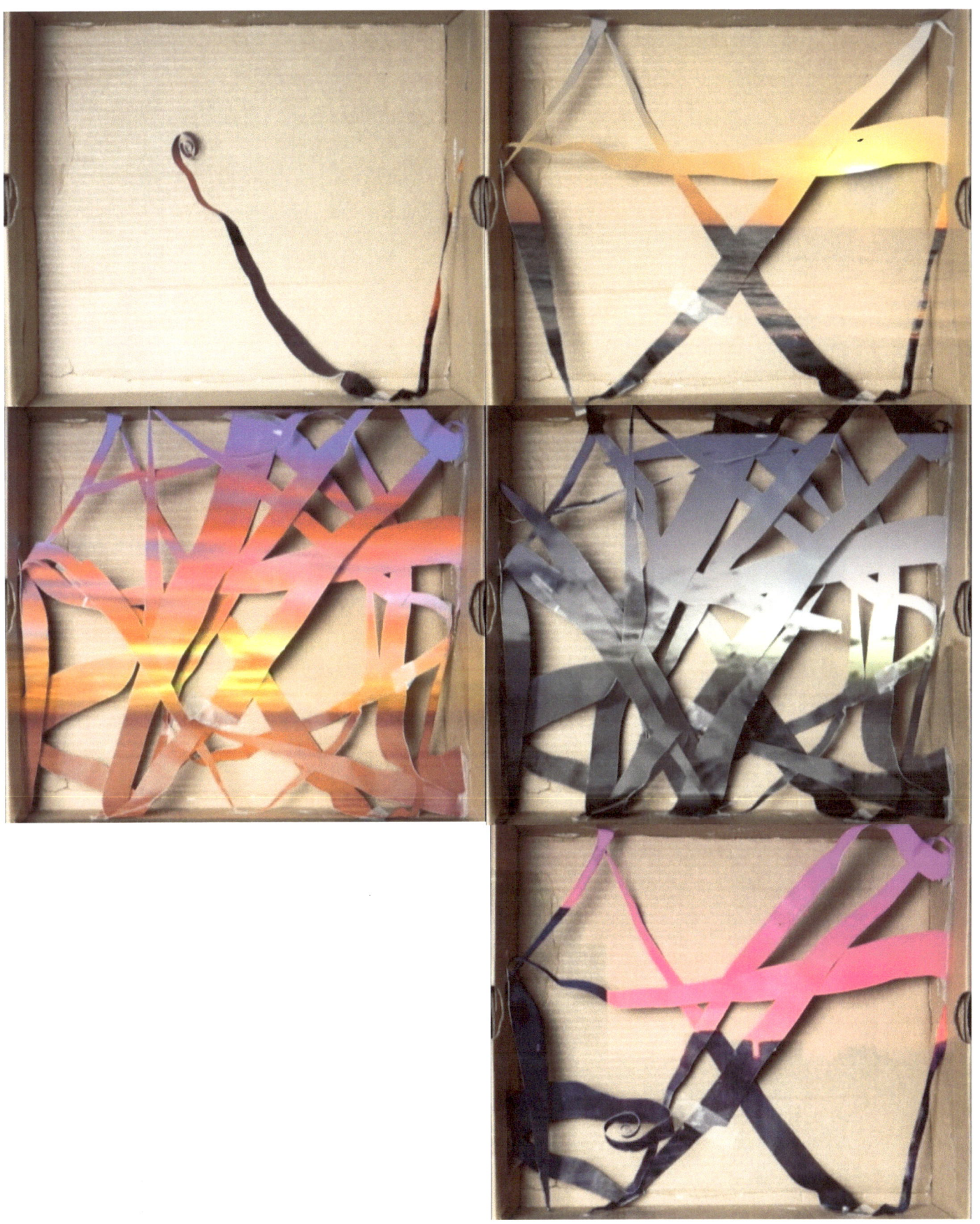

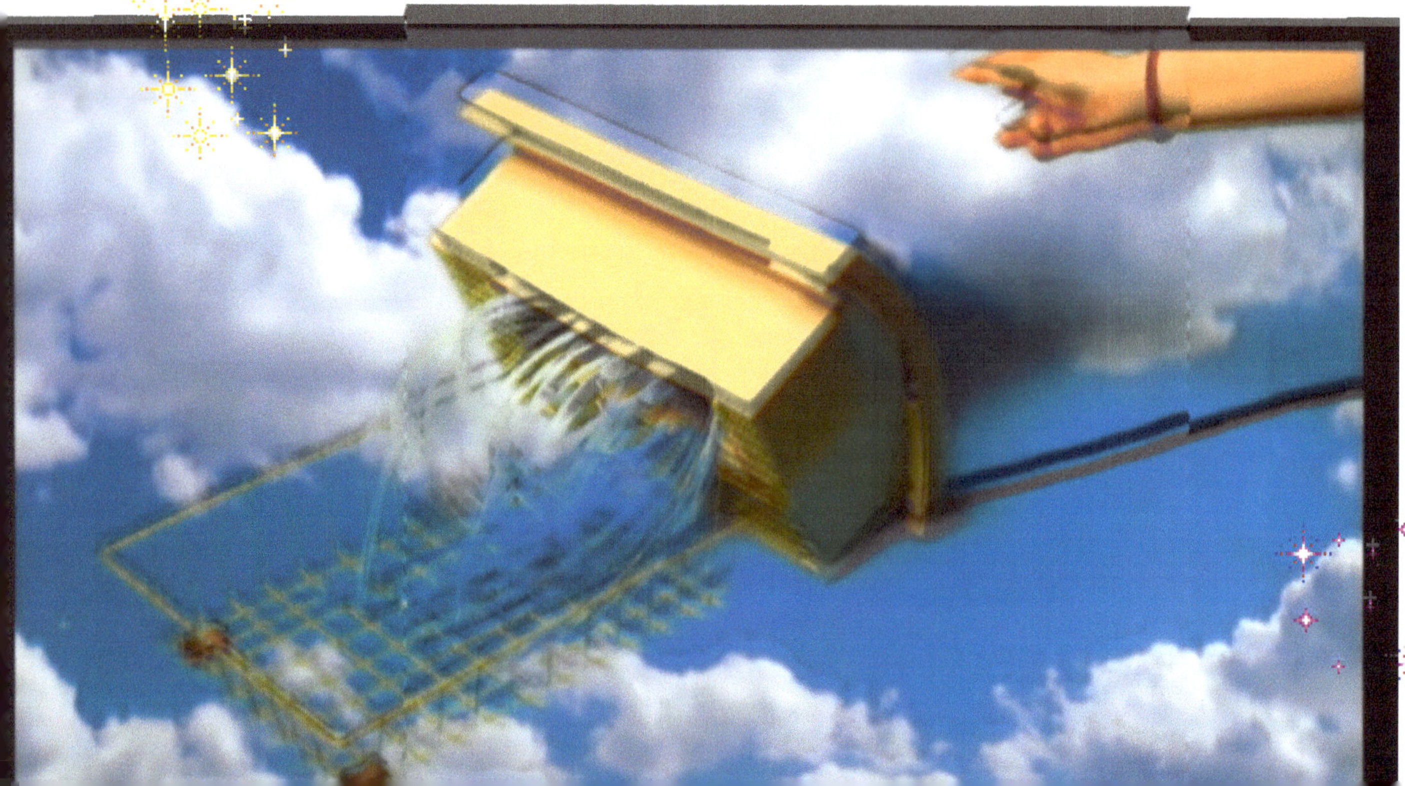

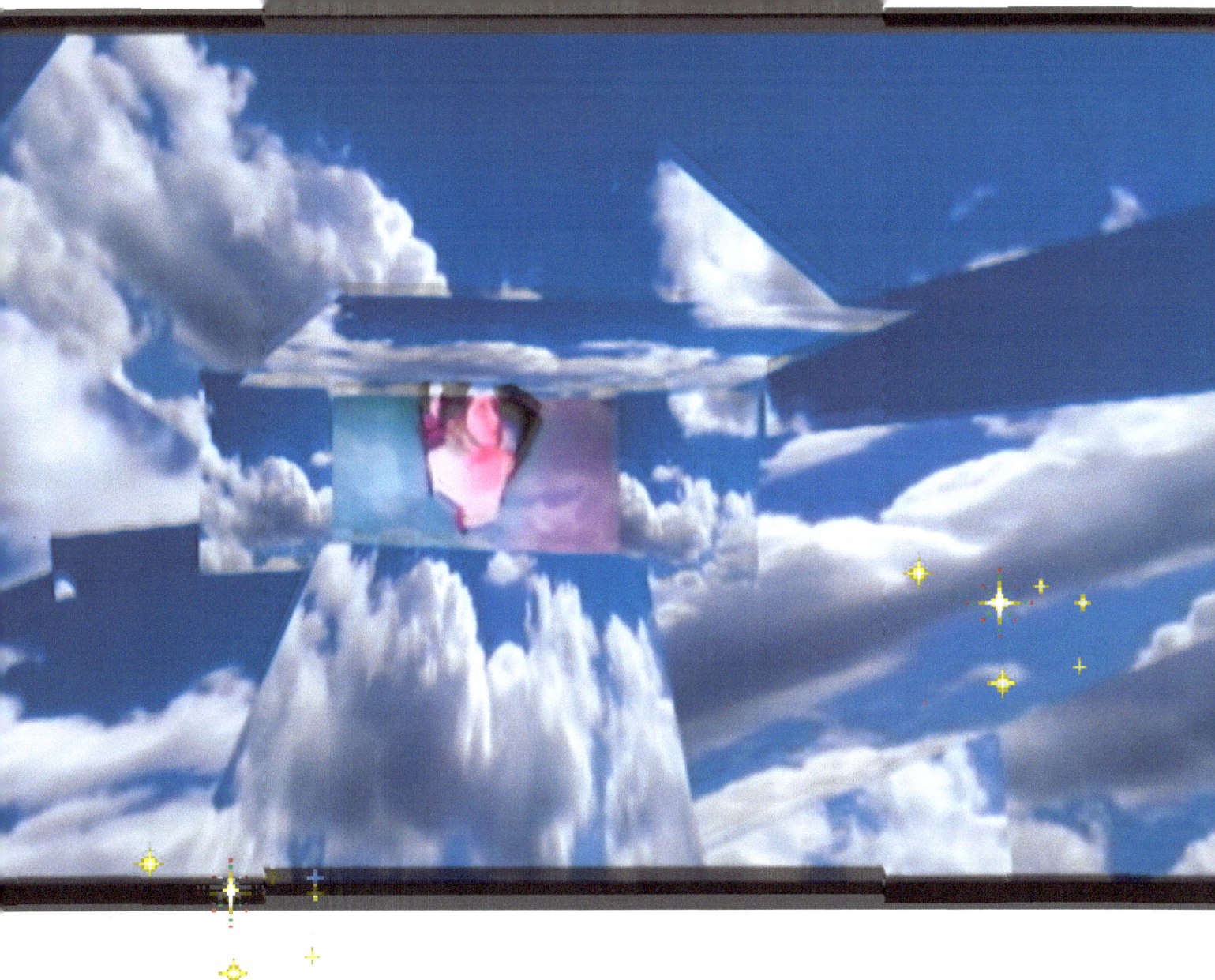

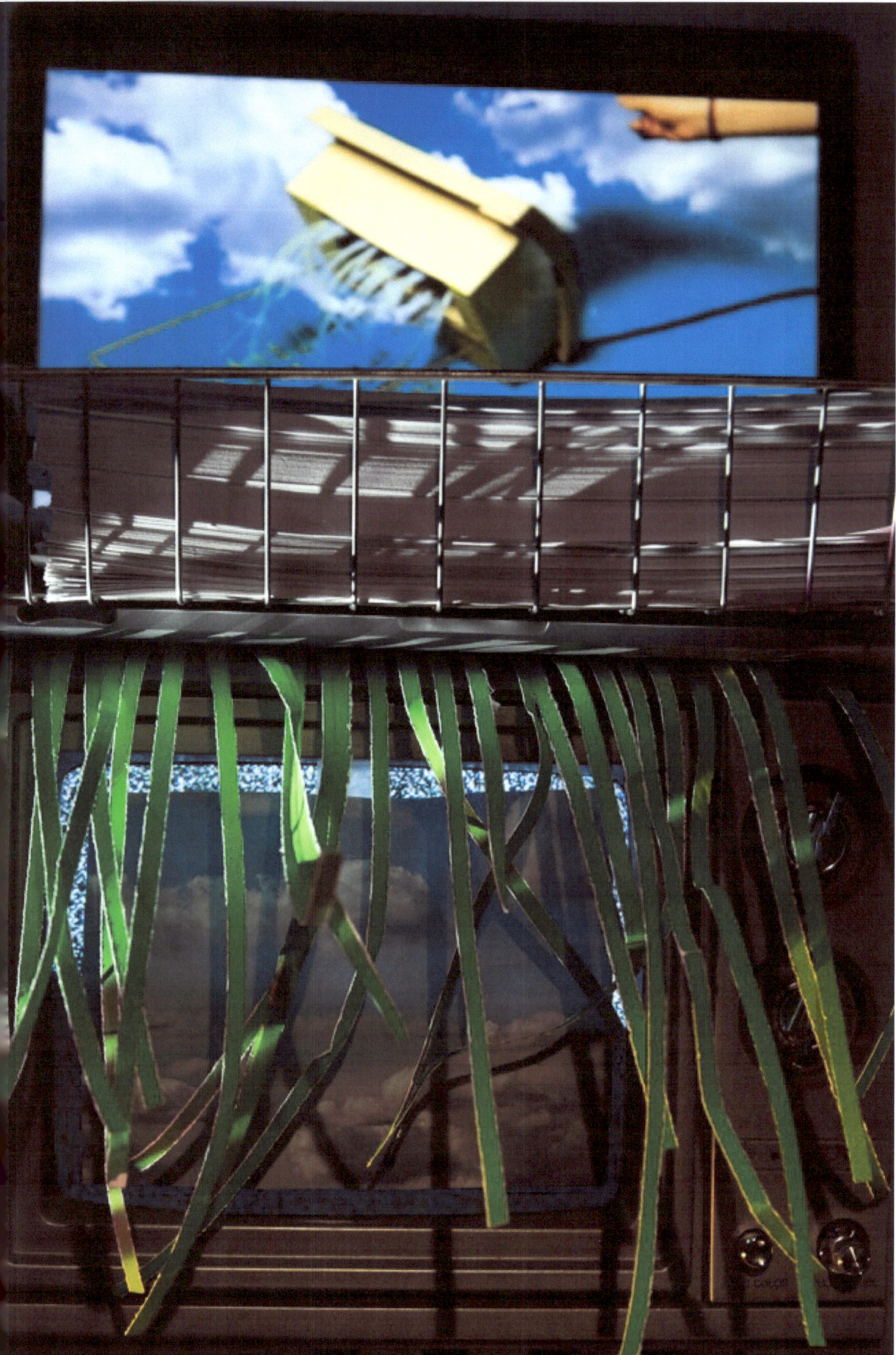

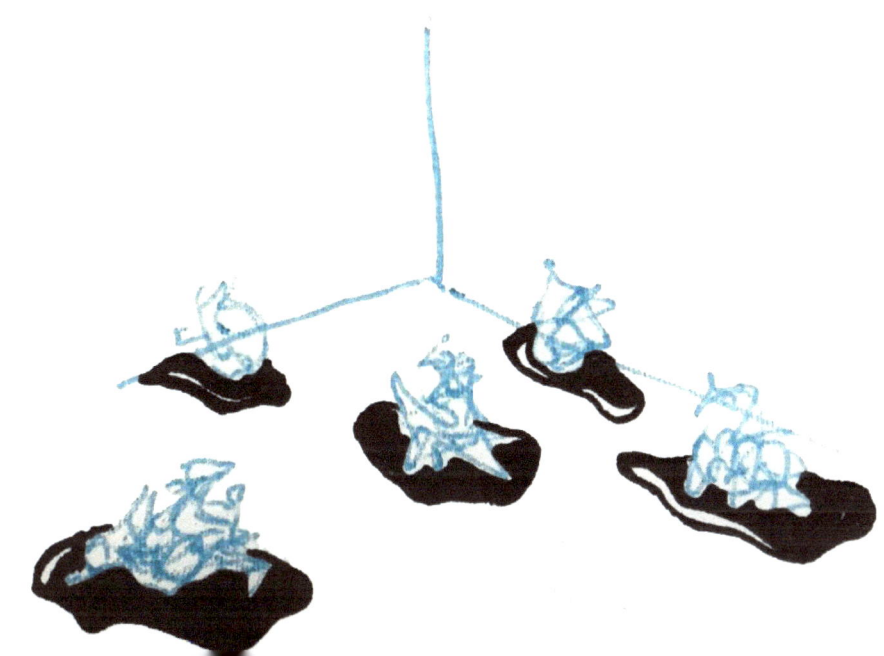

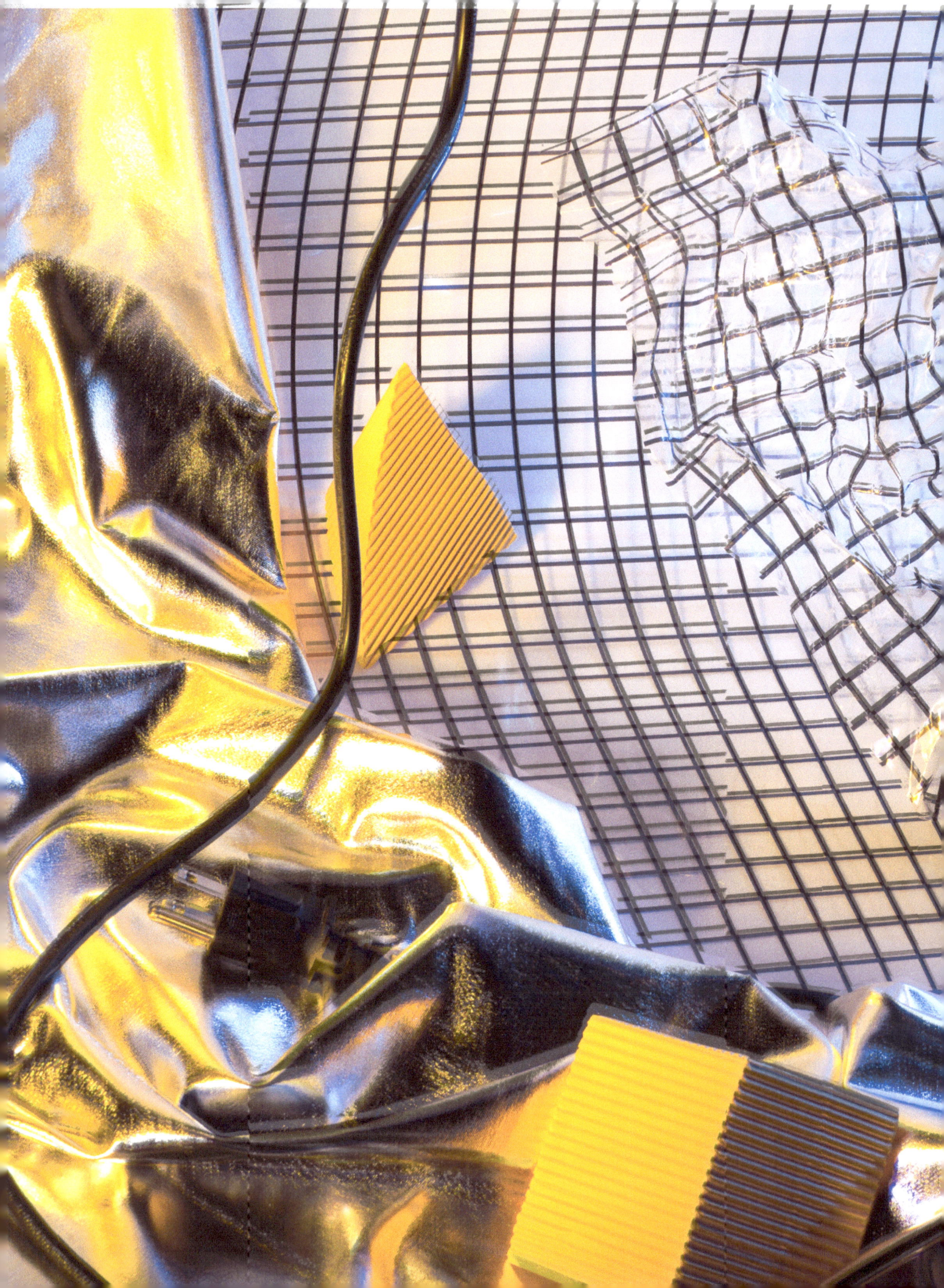

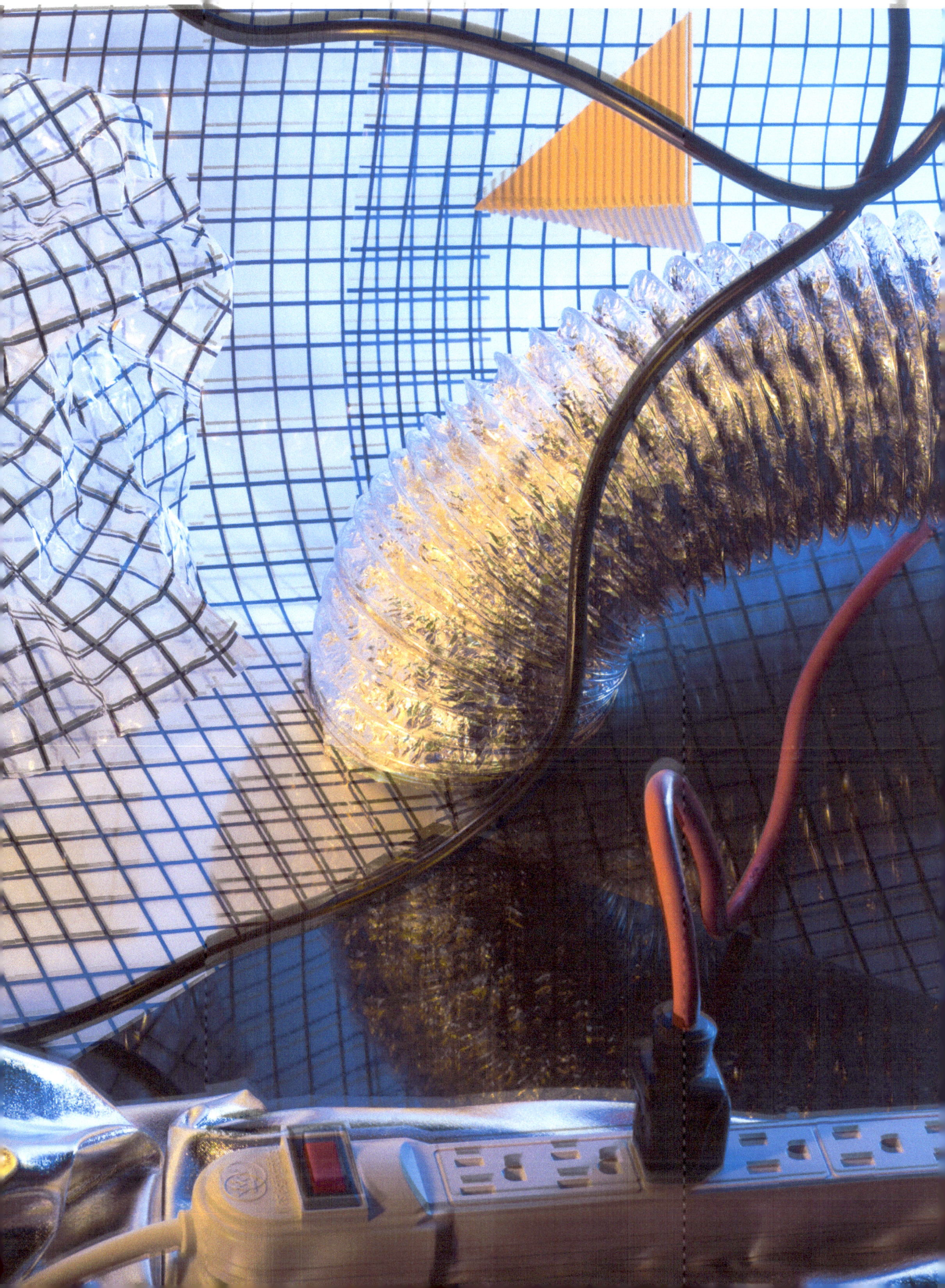

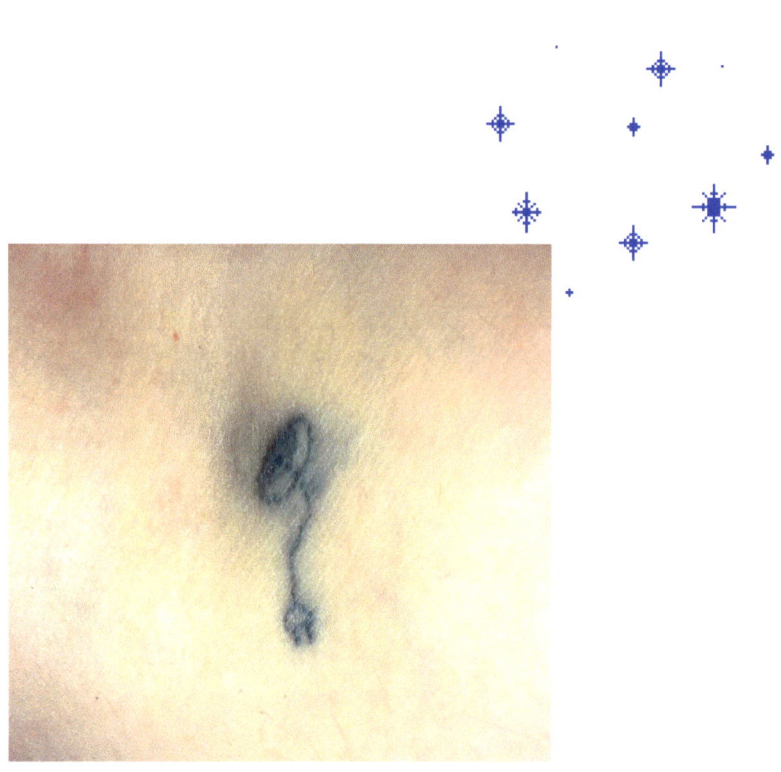

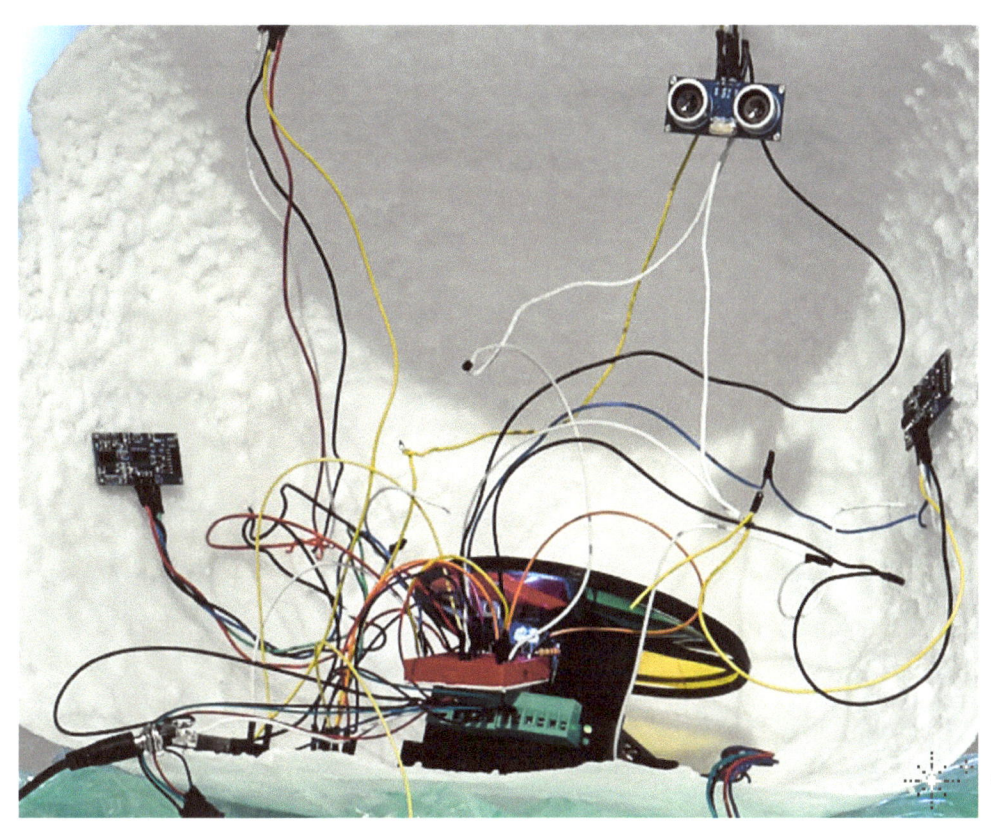

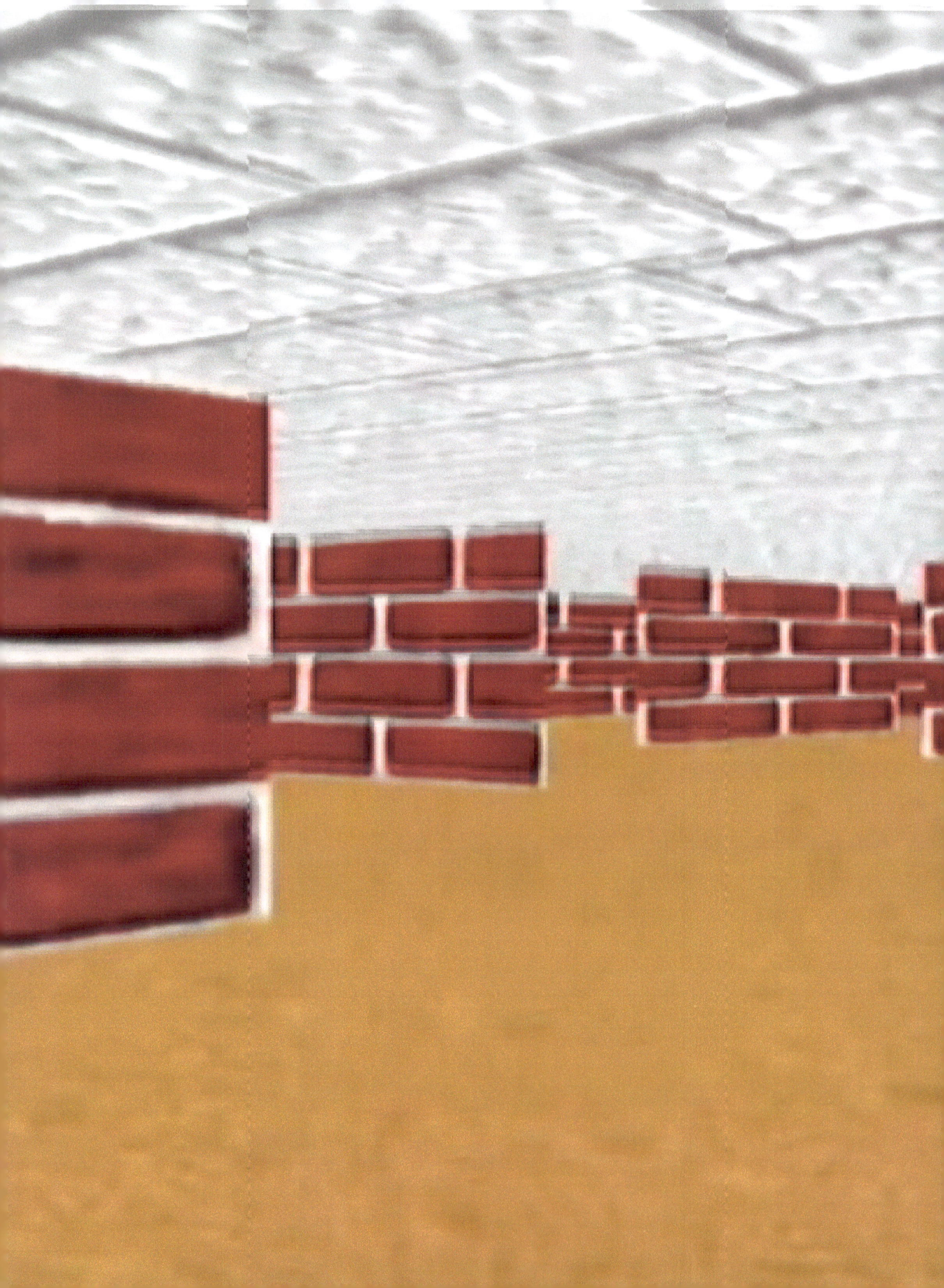

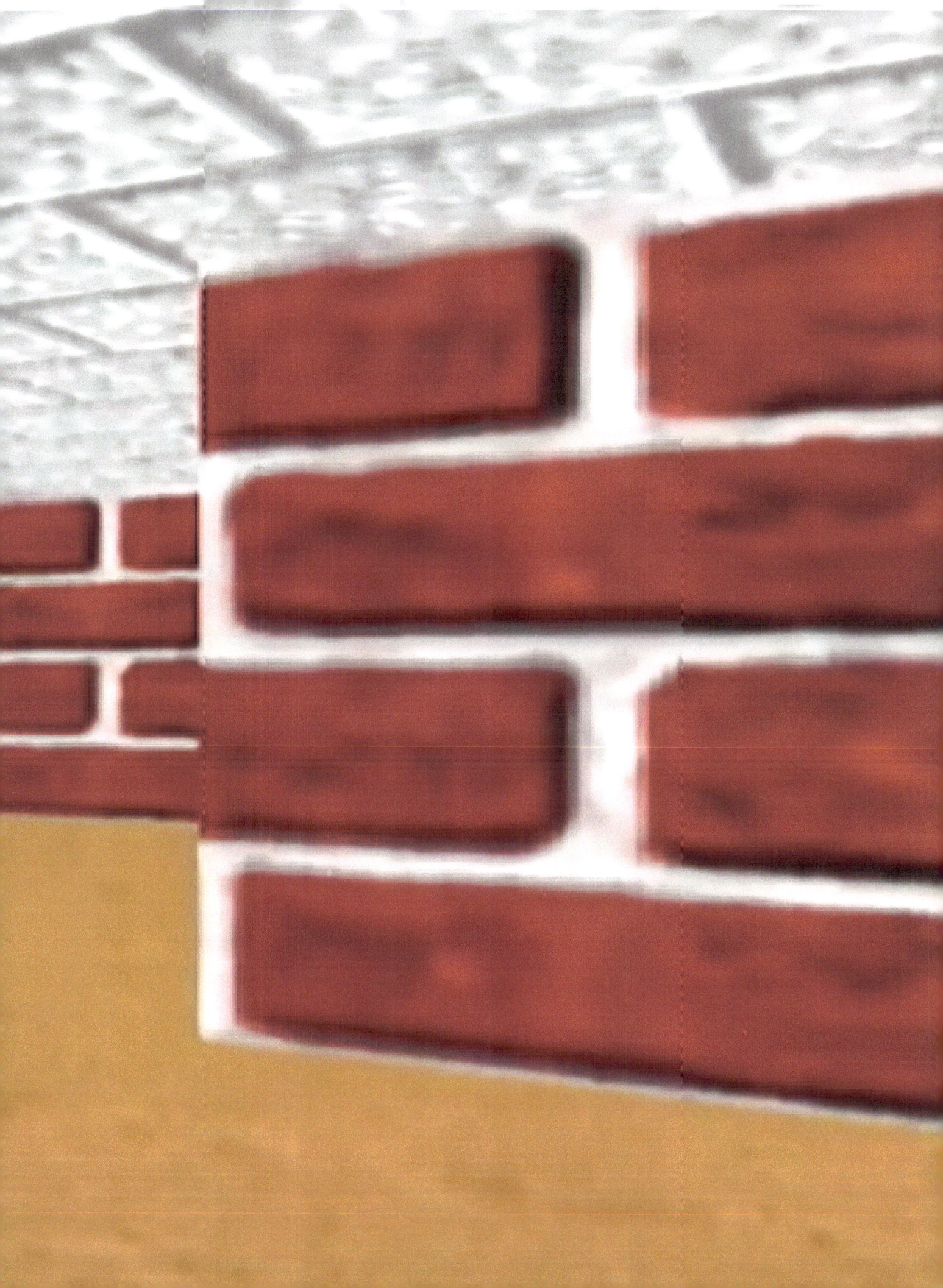

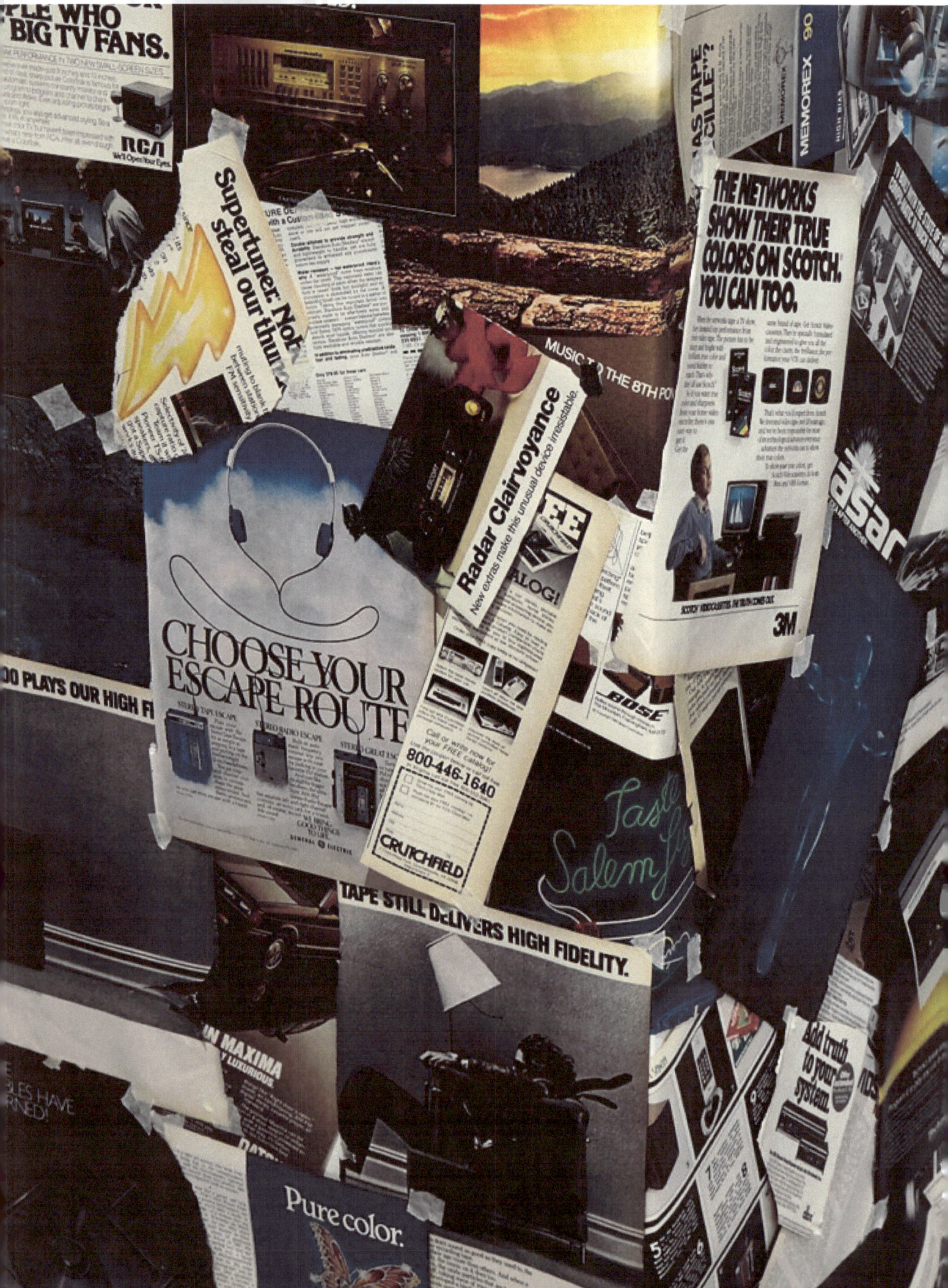

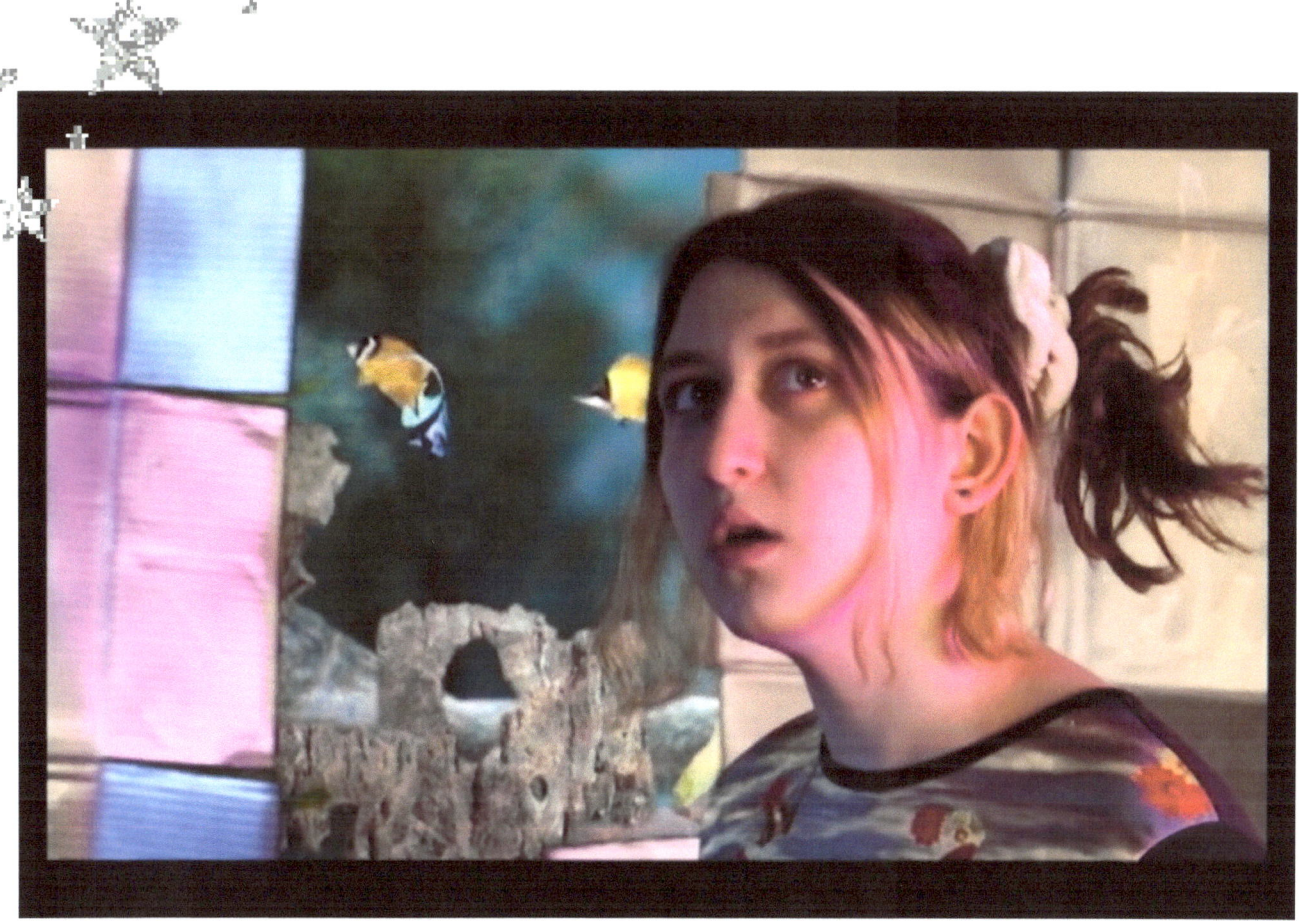

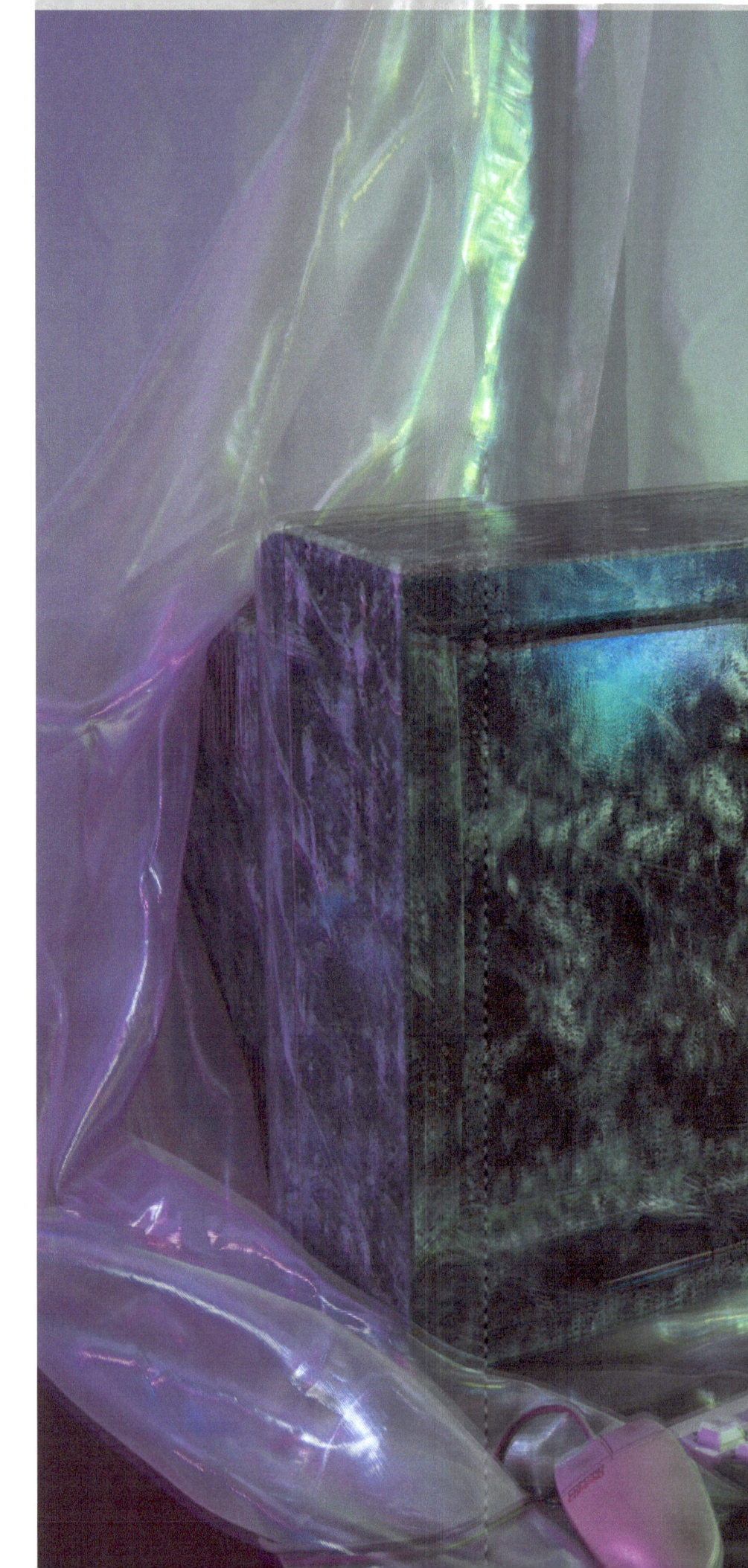

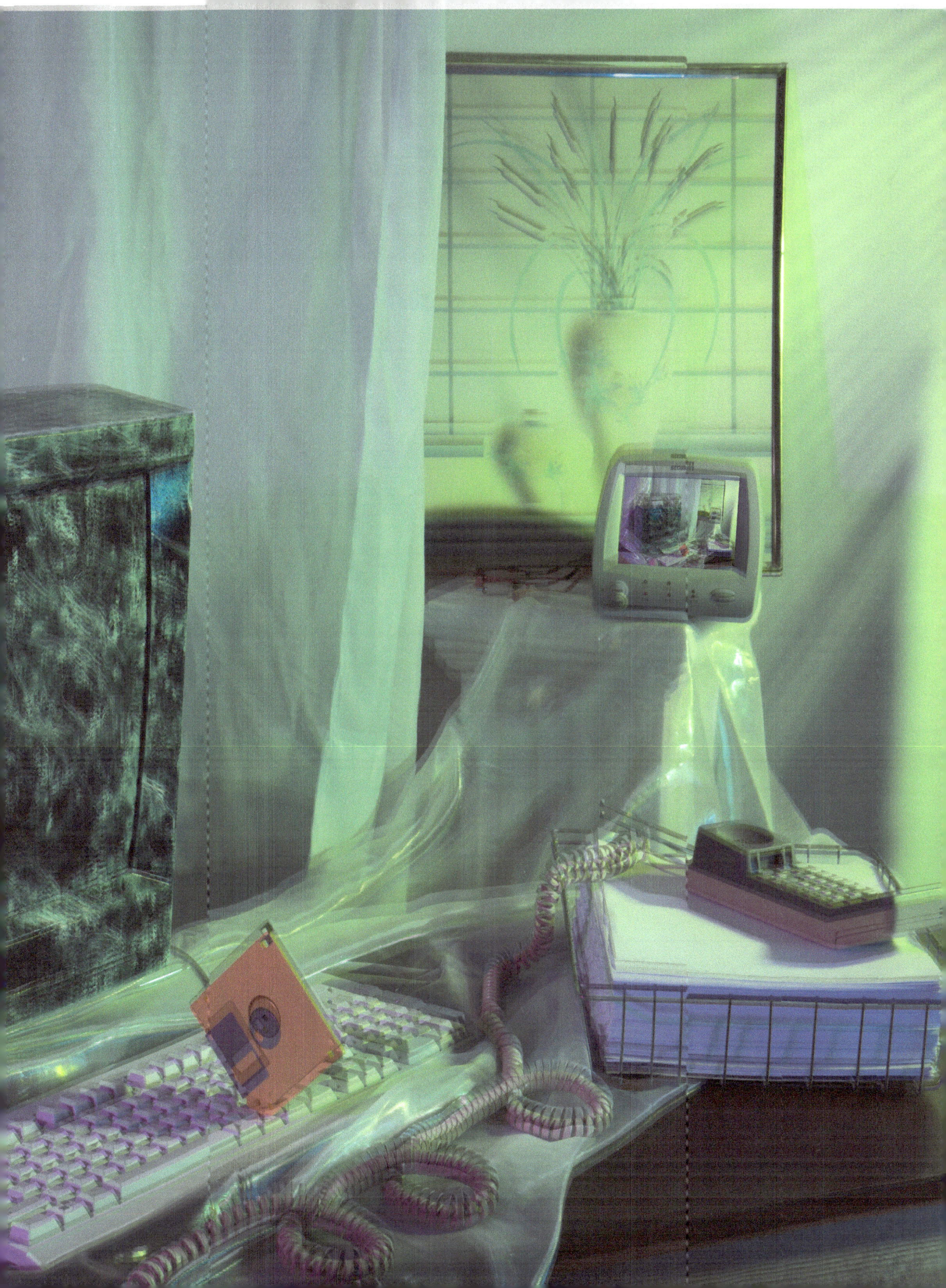

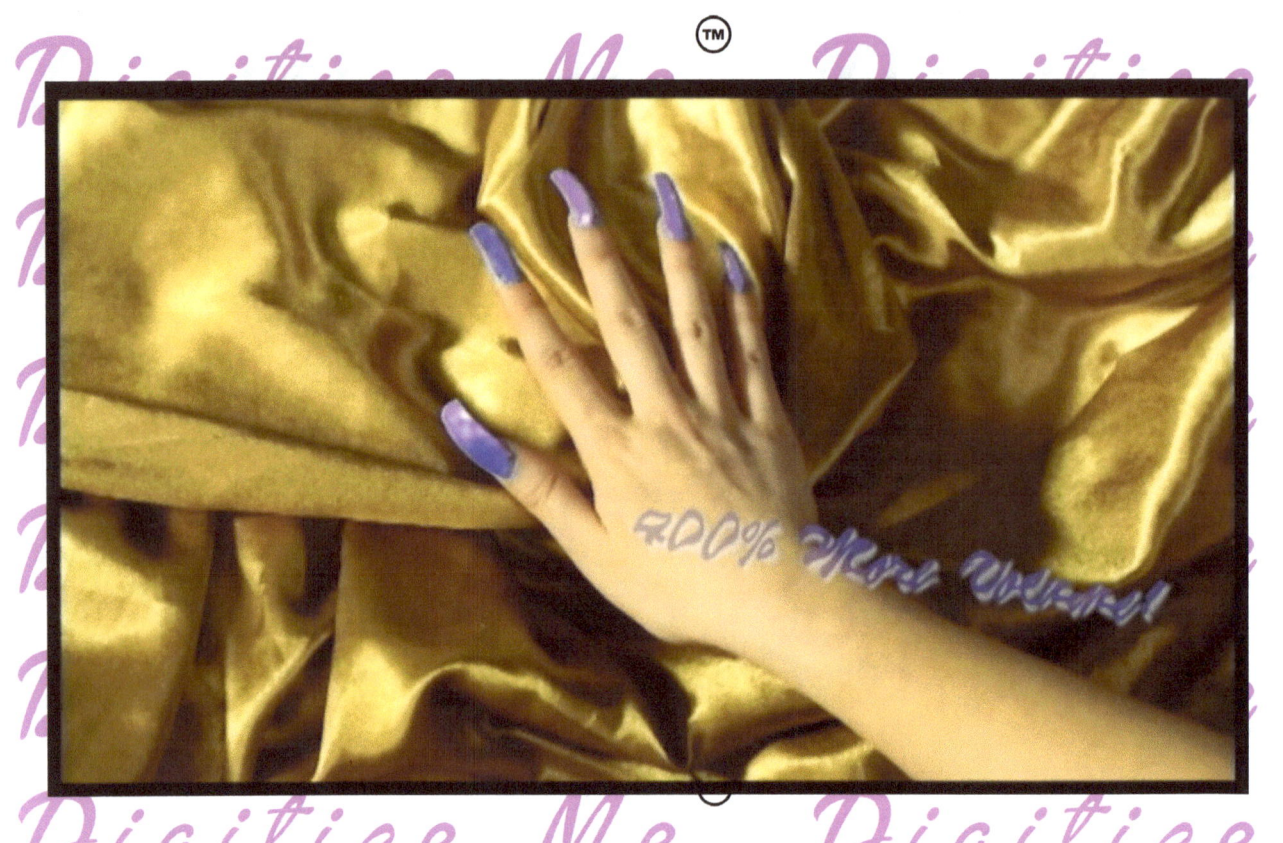

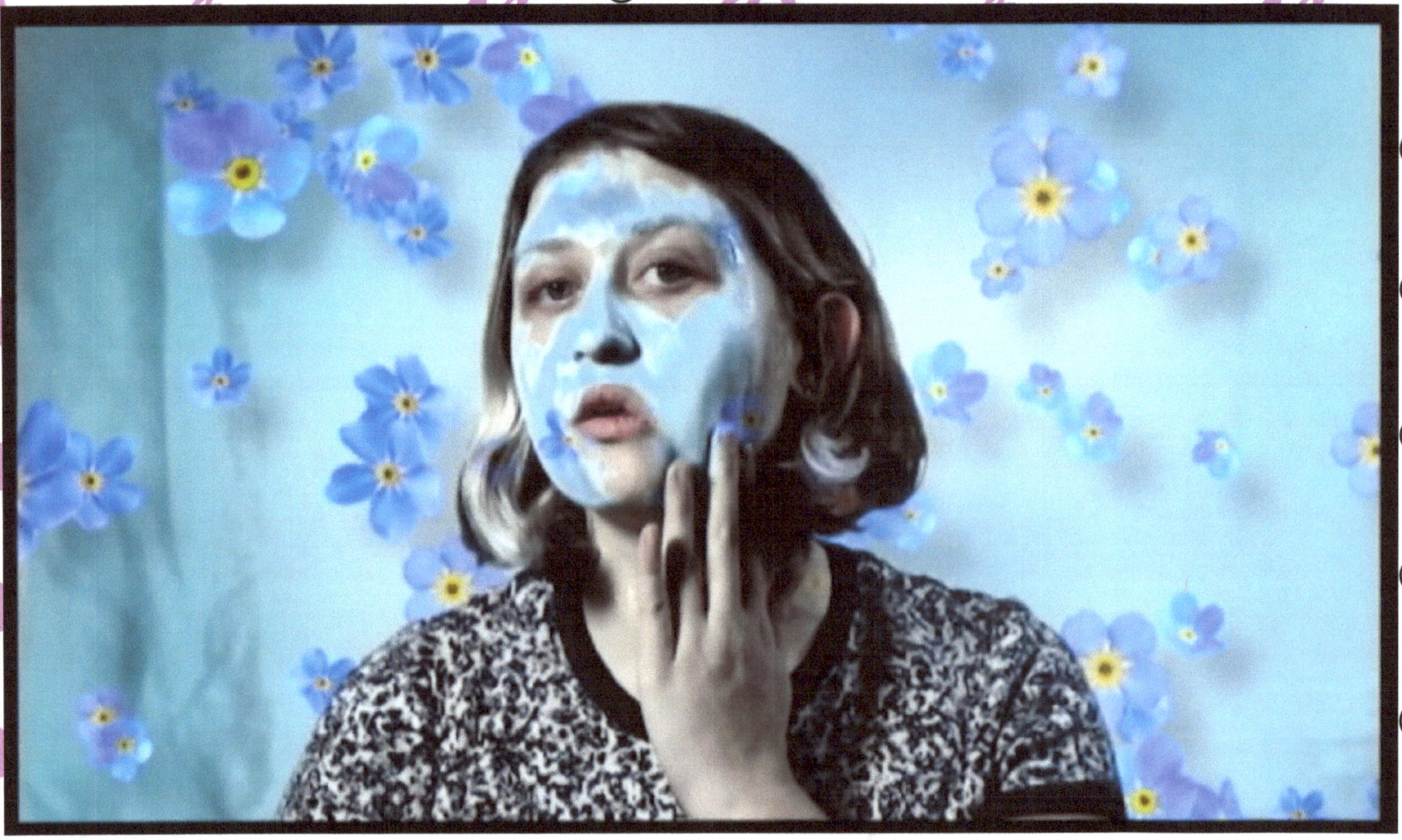

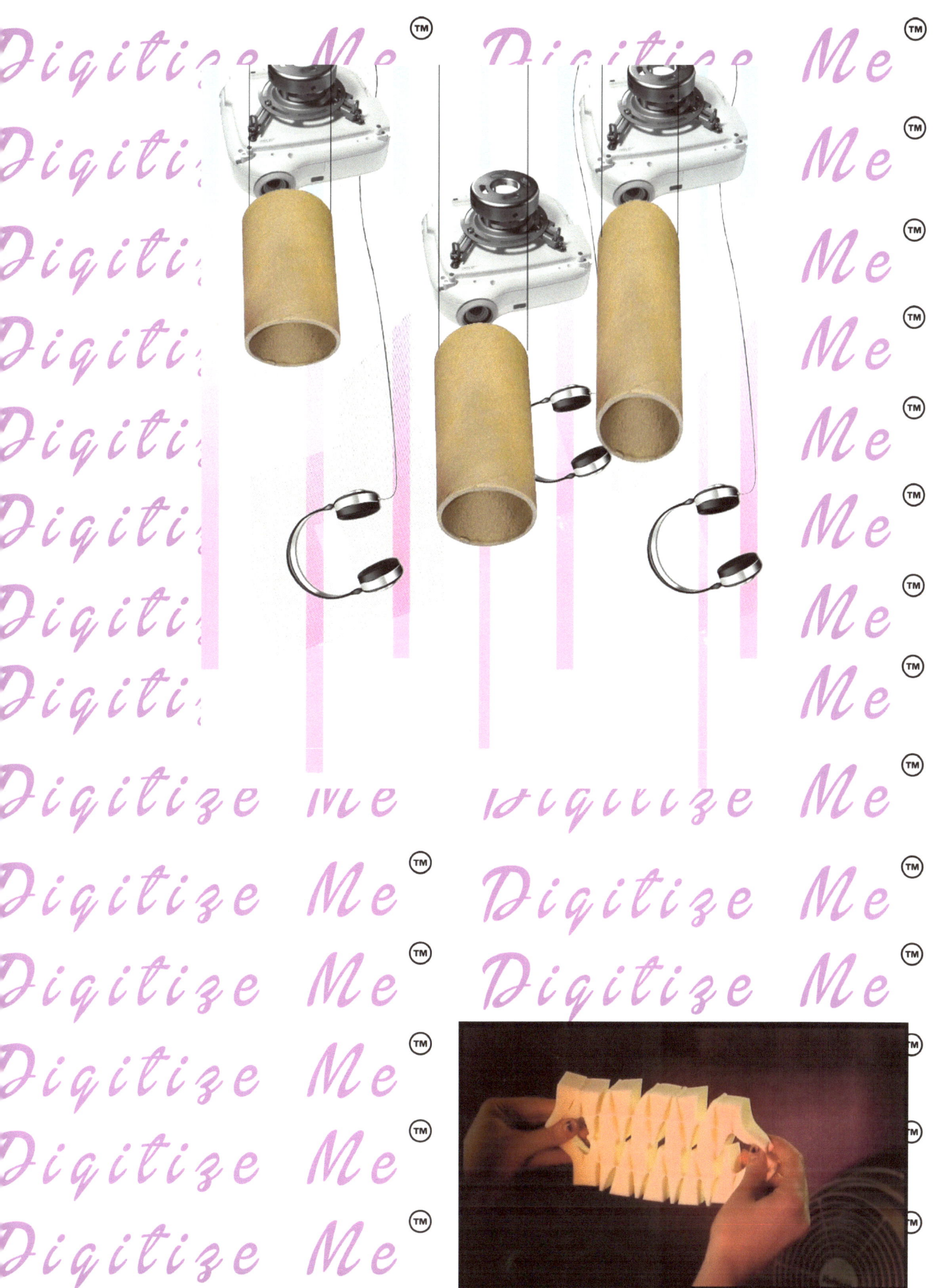

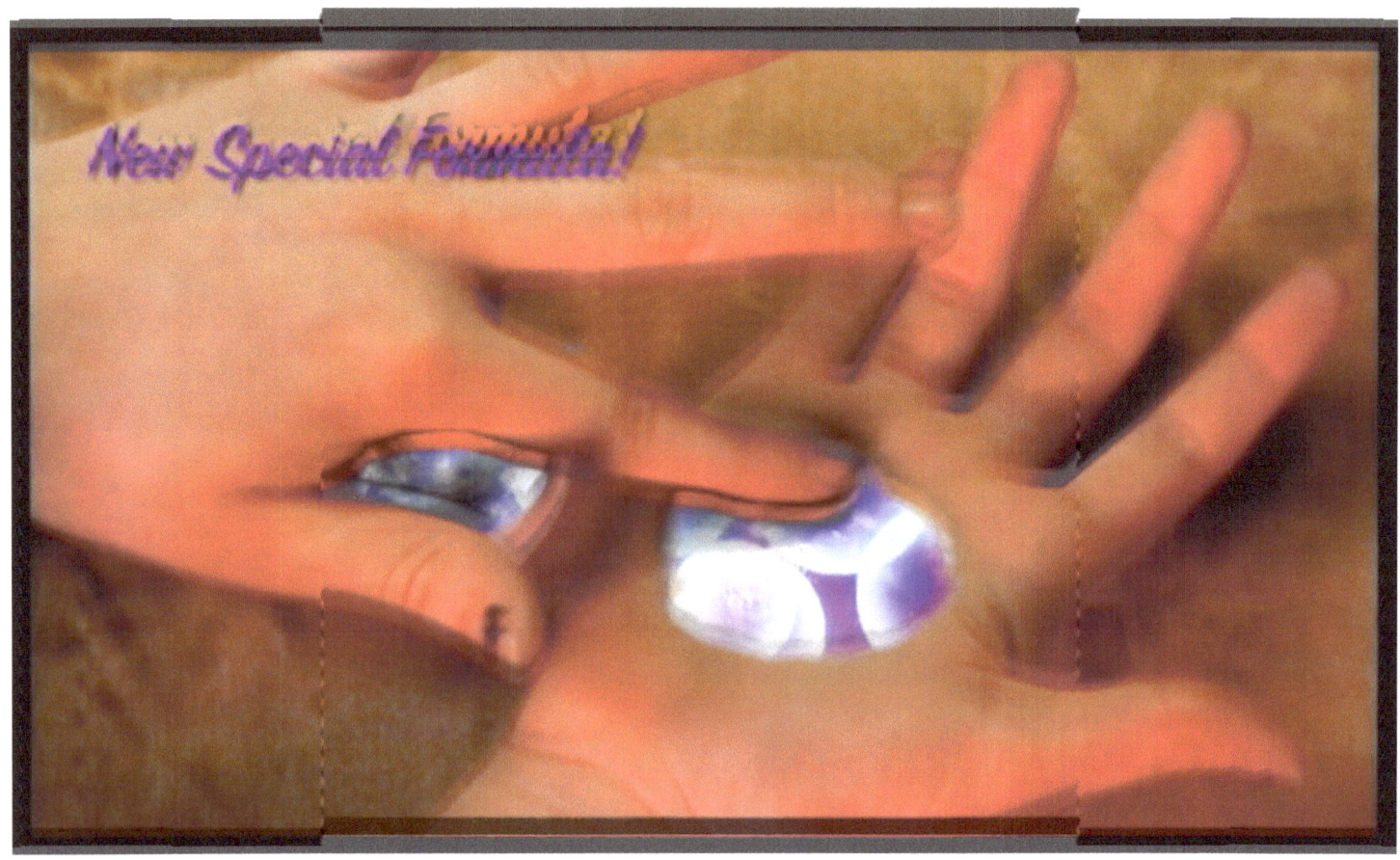

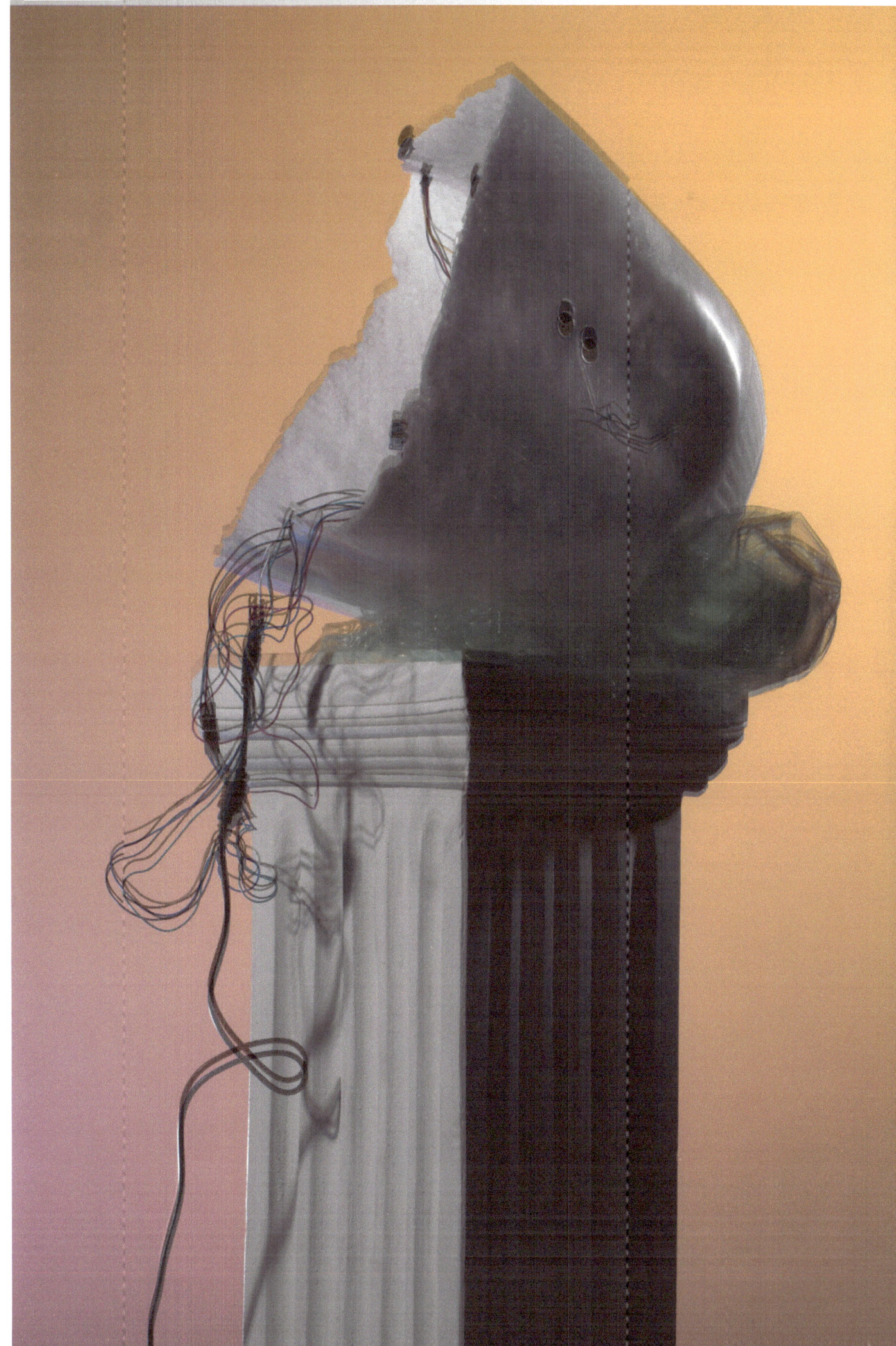

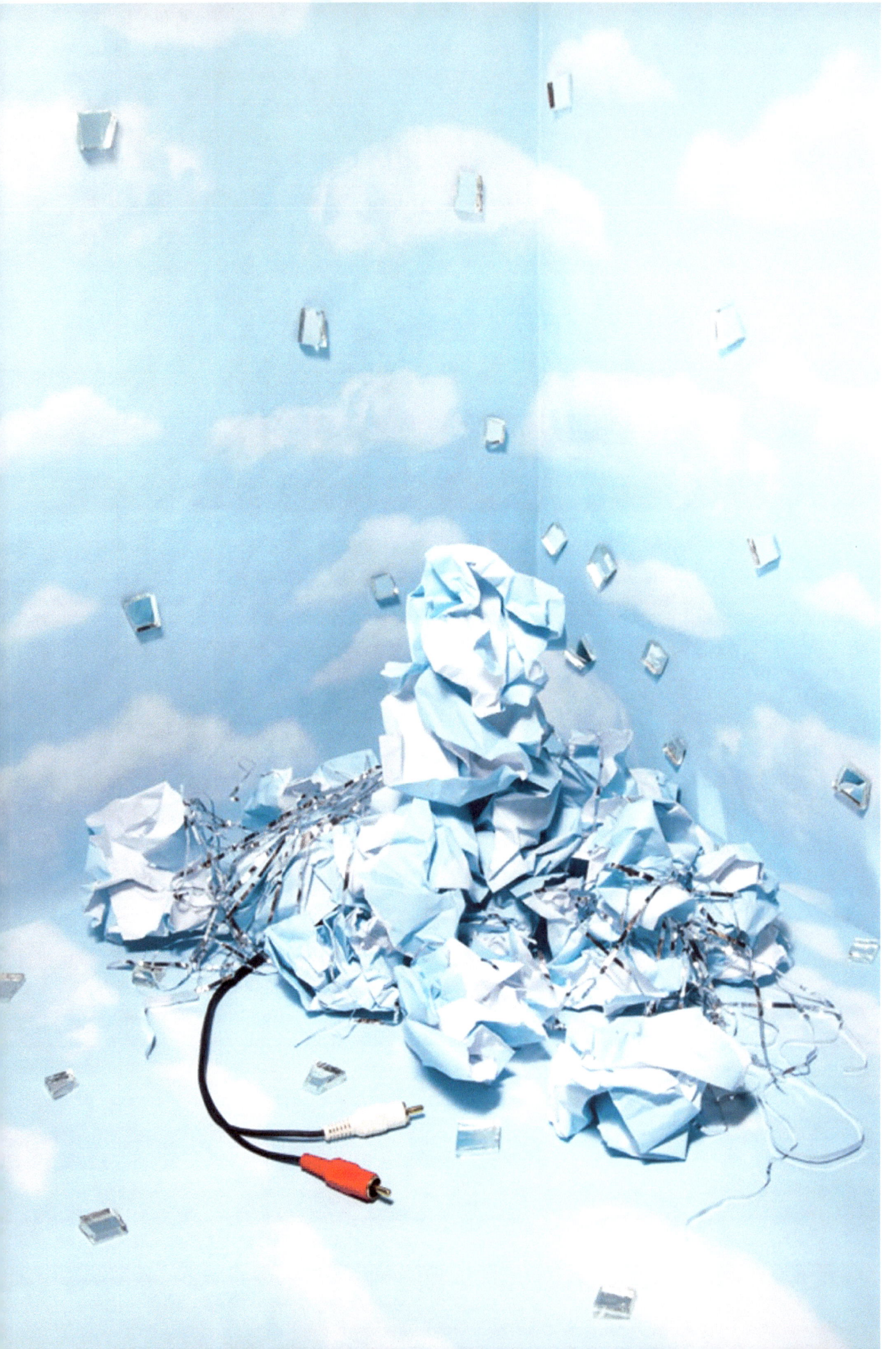

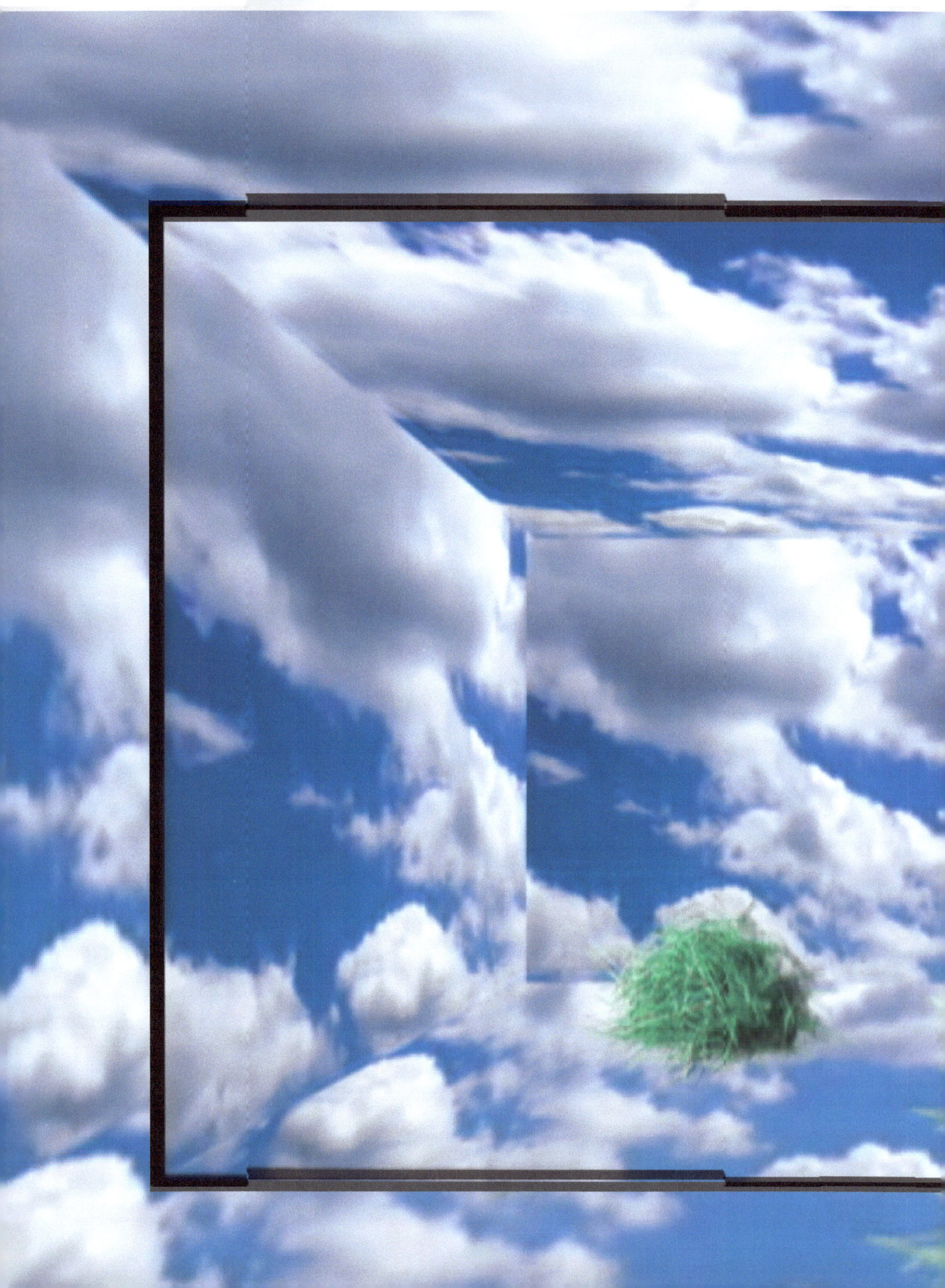

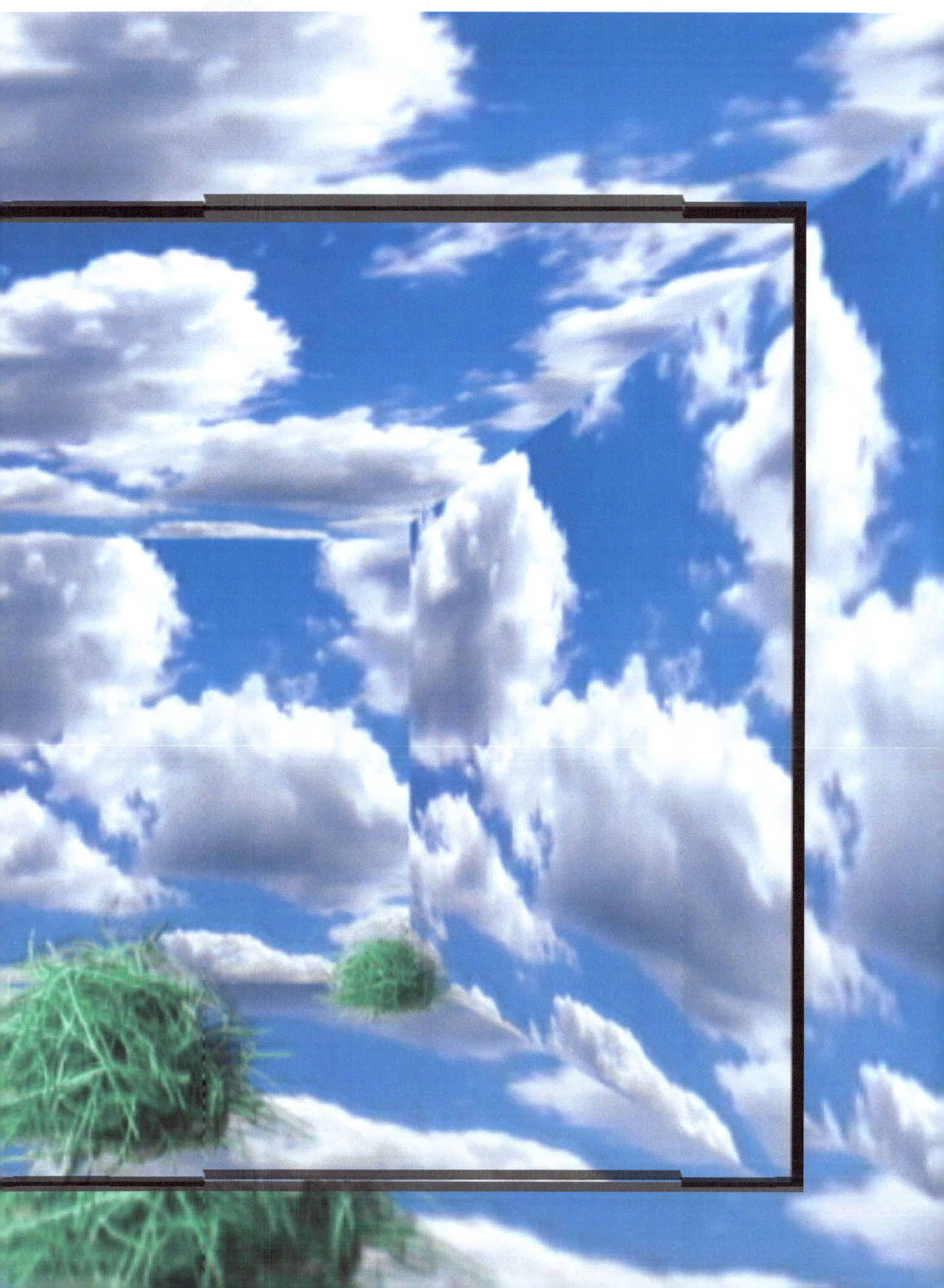

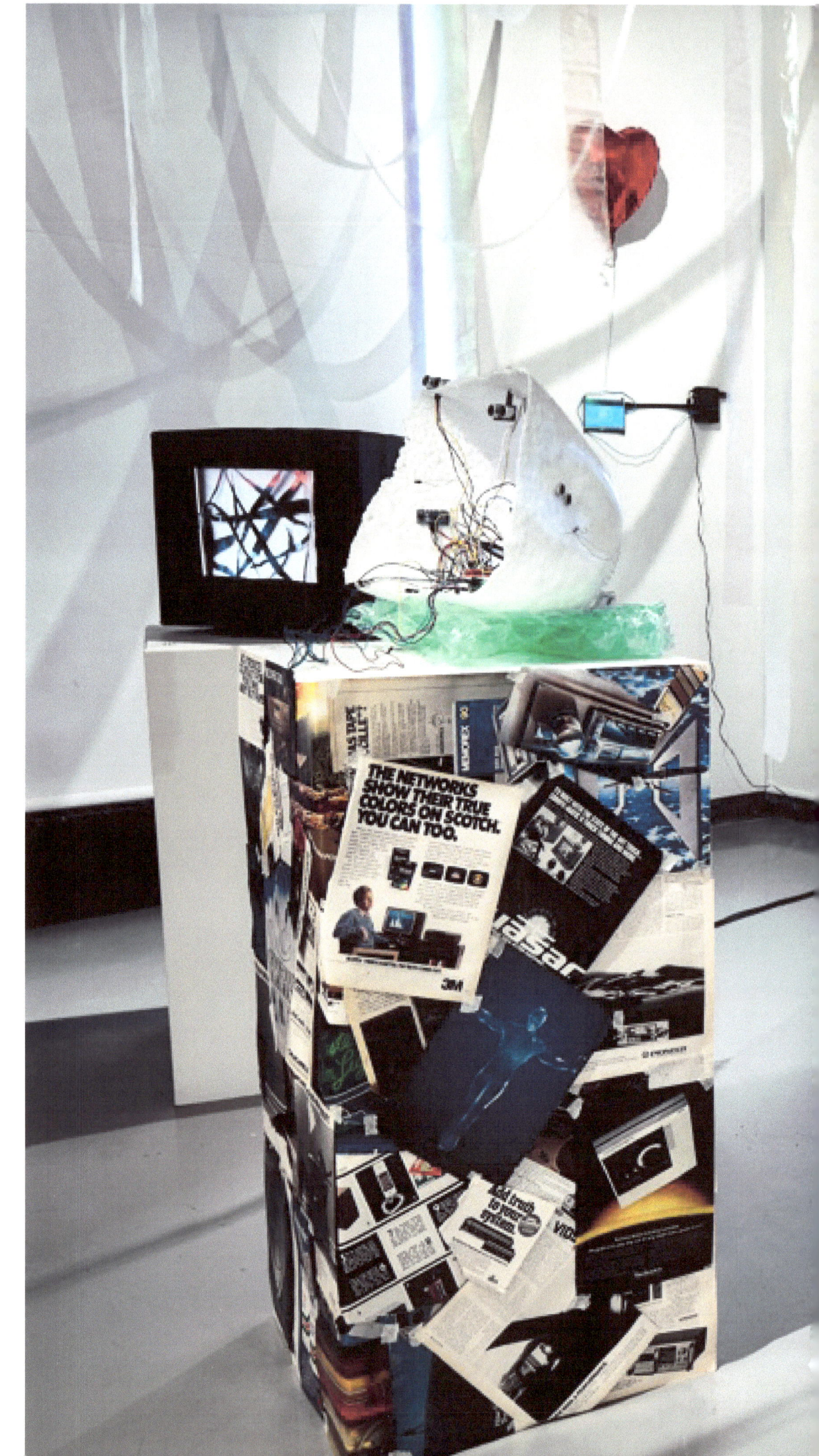

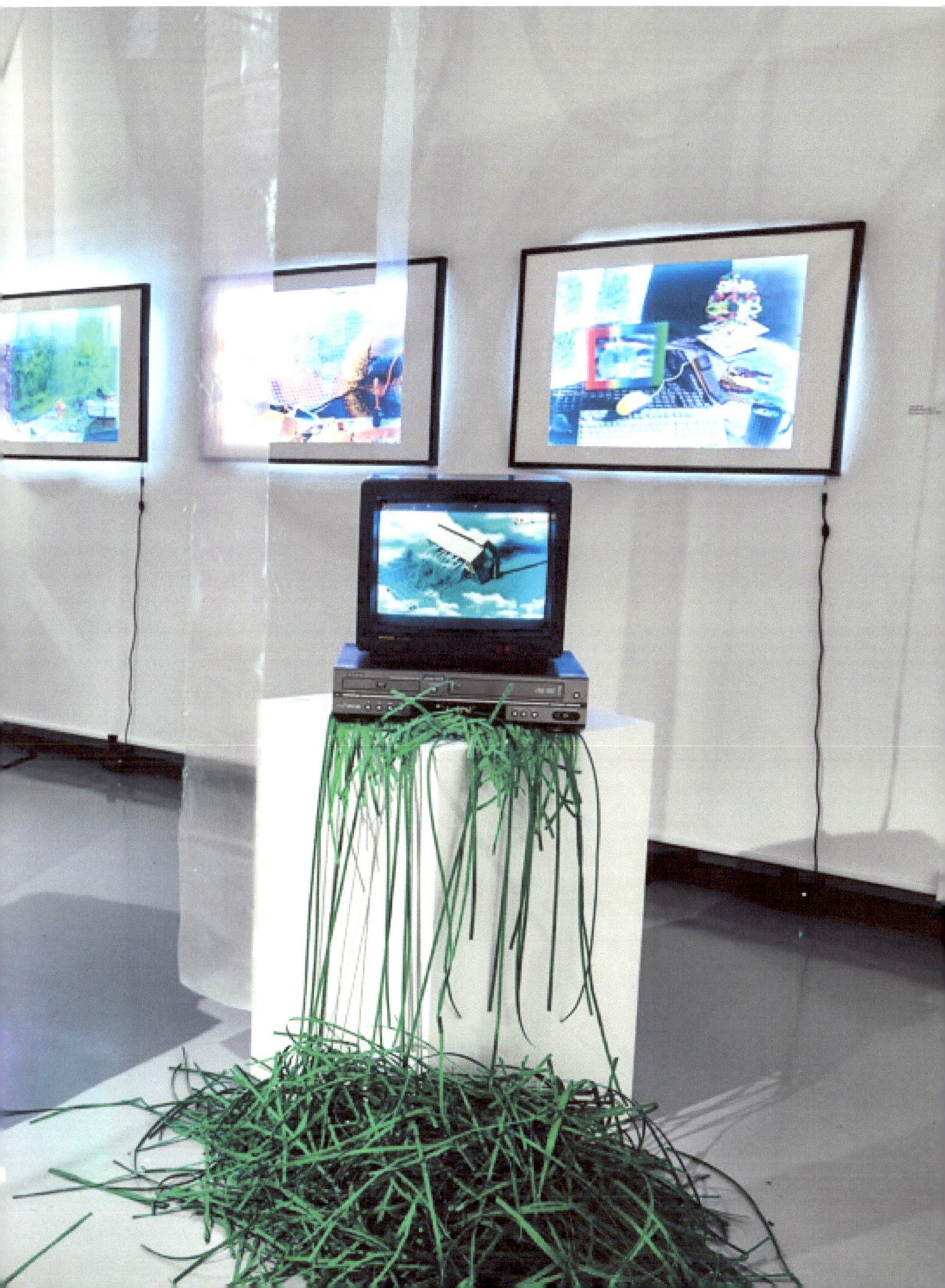

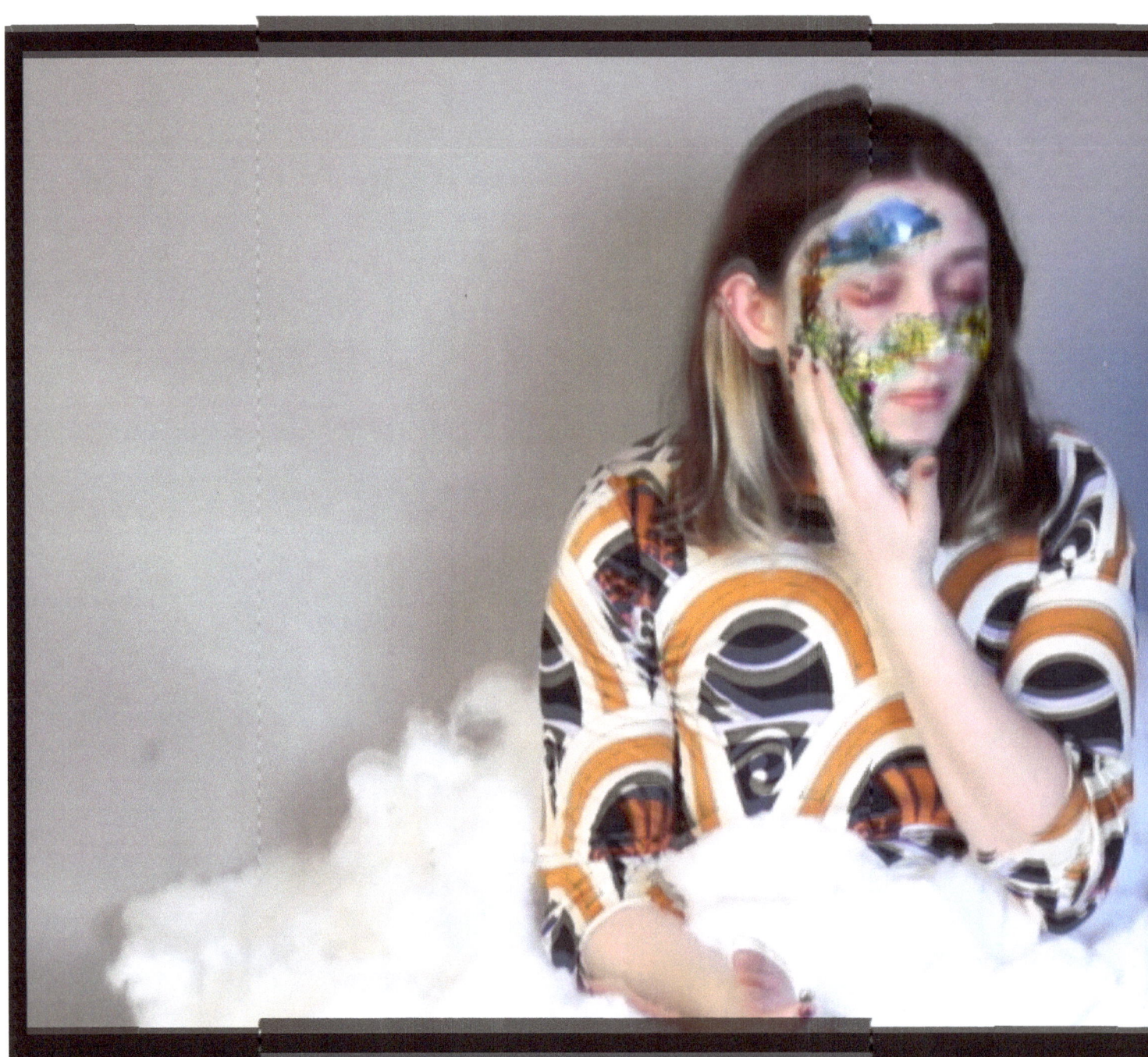

This book was produced in partial fulfillment of the Fine Art Photography undergraduate degree at the Rochester Institute of Technology.

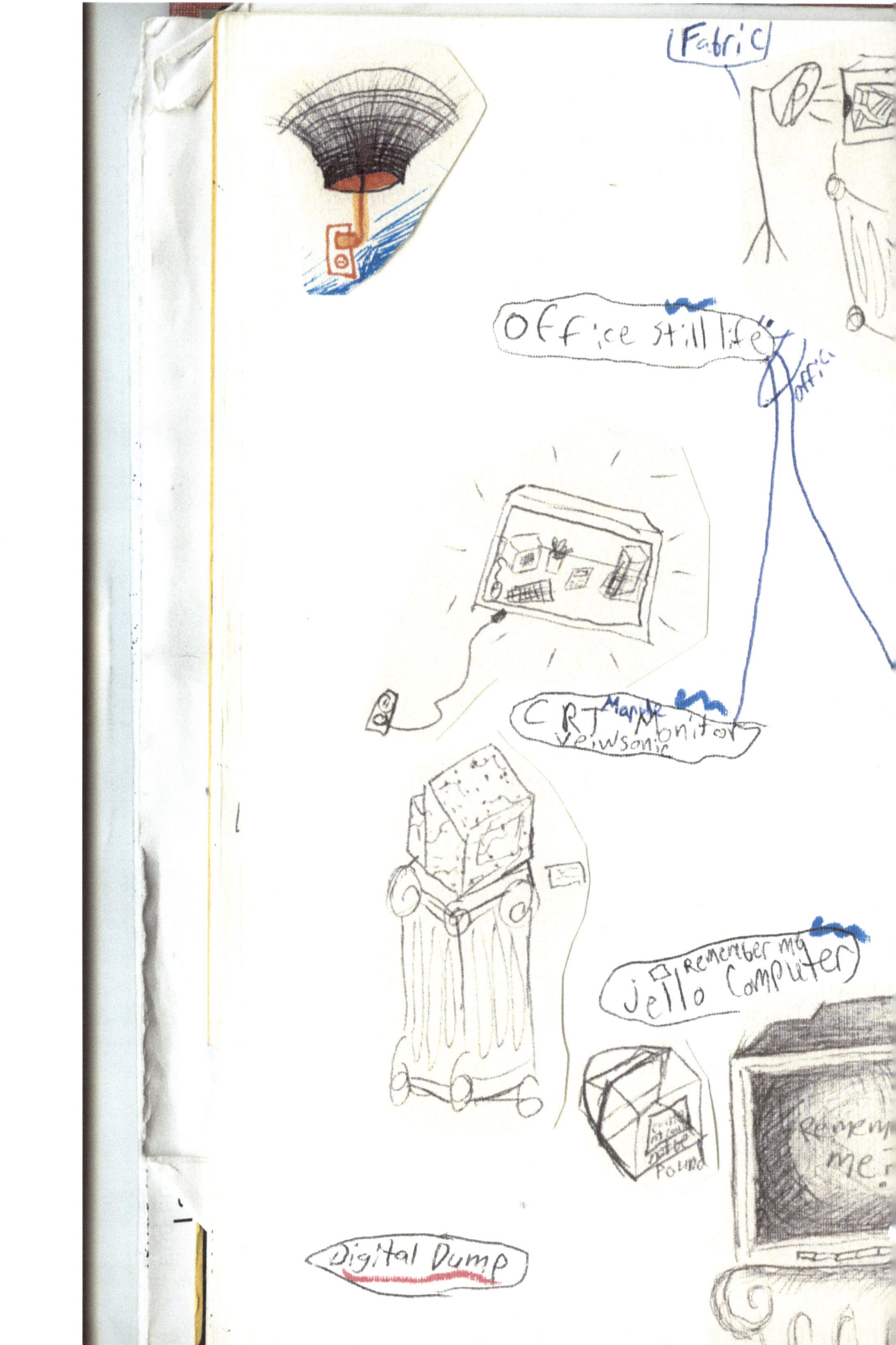

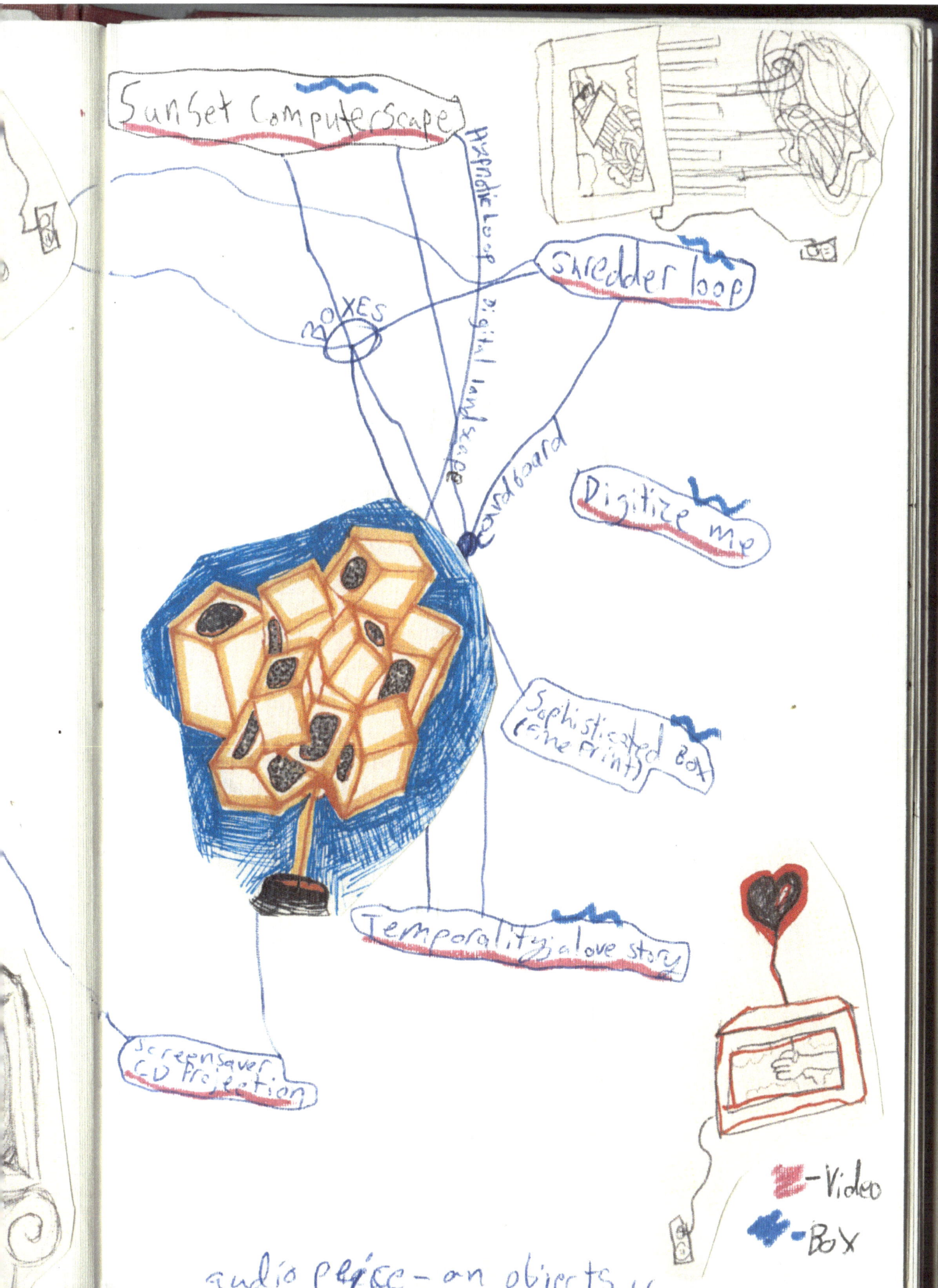

www.ingramcontent.com/pod-product-compliance
Lightning Source LLC
Chambersburg PA
CBHW051933210526
45473CB00006B/2235